TIMED READINGS PLUS

25 Two-Part Lessons
with Questions for
Building Reading Speed and Comprehension

BOOK FIVE

Edward Spargo

JAMESTOWN  PUBLISHERS

a division of NTC/CONTEMPORARY PUBLISHING GROUP
Lincolnwood, Illinois USA

Timed Readings Plus, Book Five, Level H

ISBN: 0-89061-907-7

Published by Jamestown Publishers,
a division of NTC/Contemporary Publishing Group, Inc.,
4255 West Touhy Avenue,
Lincolnwood, Illinois, 60712 U.S.A.

00 01 02 03 04 ML 10 9 8 7 6 5 4 3

CONTENTS

To the Instructor

Overview

Timed Readings Plus is designed to develop both reading speed and comprehension. A timed selection in each lesson focuses on improving reading rate. A nontimed selection—the "plus" selection—follows the timed selection. The nontimed selection concentrates on building mastery in critical areas of comprehension.

The 10 books in the series span reading levels 4–13, with one book at each level. Readability of the selections was assessed by using the Fry Readability Scale. Each book contains 25 lessons; each lesson is divided into Parts A and B.

Part A includes the timed selection followed by 10 multiple-choice questions: 5 fact questions and 5 thought questions. The timed selection is 400 words long and contains subject matter that is factual, nonfiction, and textbook-like. Because everyone—regardless of level—reads a 400-word passage, the steps for the timed selection can be concurrent for everyone.

Part B includes the nontimed selection, which is more narrative than the timed selection. The length of the selection varies depending on the subject matter, which relates to the content of the timed selection. The nontimed selection is followed by five comprehension questions that address the following major comprehension skills: recognizing words in context, distinguishing fact from opinion, keeping events in order, making correct inferences, and understanding main ideas.

Getting Started

Begin by assigning students to a level. A student should start with a book that is one level below his or her current reading level. If a student's reading level is not known, a suitable starting point would be one or two levels below the student's present grade in school.

Teaching a Lesson: Part A

Work in each lesson begins with the timed selection in Part A. If you wish to have all the students in the class read a selection at the same time, you can coordinate the timing using the following method. Give students the signal to preview. Allow 15 seconds for this. Have students begin reading the selection at the same time. After one minute has passed, write on the chalkboard the time that has elapsed. Update the time at 10-second intervals (1:00, 1:10, 1:20, etc.). Tell students to copy down the last time shown on the chalkboard when they finish reading. They should then record this reading time in the space designated after the selection.

If students keep track of their own reading times, have them write the times at which they start and finish reading on a separate piece of paper and then figure and record their reading time as above.

Students should now answer the ten questions that follow the Part A selection. Responses are recorded by putting an X in the box next to the student's choice of answer. Correct responses to eight or more questions indicates satisfactory comprehension and recall.

Teaching a Lesson: Part B

When students have finished Part A, they can move on to read the Part B selection. Although brief, these selections deliver all the content needed to attack the range of comprehension questions that follow.

Students next answer the comprehension questions that follow the Part B selection. Directions for answering the questions are provided with each question. Correct responses require deliberation and discrimination.

Correcting and Scoring Answers

Using the Answer Key at the back of the book, students self-score their responses to the questions in Parts A and B. Incorrect answers should be circled and the correct answers should be marked. The number of correct answers for Part A and for Part B and the total correct answers should be tallied on the final page of the lesson.

Using the Graphs

Reading times are plotted on the Reading Rate graph at the back of the book. The legend on the graph automatically converts reading times to words-per-minute rates. Comprehension totals are plotted on the Comprehension Scores graph. Plotting automatically converts the raw scores to a comprehension percentage based on four points per correct answer.

Diagnosis and Evaluation

The Comprehension Skills Profile graph at the back of the book tracks student responses to the Part B comprehension questions. For each incorrect response, students should mark an X in the corresponding box on the graph. A column of Xs rising above other columns indicates a specific comprehension weakness. Using the profile, you can assess trends in student performance and suggest remedial work if necessary.

A student who has reached a peak in reading speed (with satisfactory comprehension) is ready to advance to the next book in the series. Before moving on to the next book, students should be encouraged to maintain their speed and comprehension on a number of lessons in order to consolidate their achievement.

How to Use This Book

Getting Started

Study Part A: Reading Faster and Better. Read and learn the steps to follow and the techniques to use to help you read more quickly and more efficiently.

Study Part B: Mastering Reading Comprehension. Learn what the five categories of comprehension are all about. Knowing what kind of comprehension response is expected from you and how to achieve that response will help you better comprehend all you read.

Working a Lesson

Find the Starting Lesson. Locate the timed selection in Part A of the lesson that you are going to read. Wait for your instructor's signal to preview the selection. Your instructor will allow you 15 seconds for previewing.

Read the Part A Selection. When your instructor gives you the signal, begin reading. Read at a faster-than-normal speed. Read carefully so that you will be able to answer questions about what you have read.

Record Your Reading Time. When you finish reading, look at the blackboard and note your reading time. Write this time at the bottom of the page on the line labeled Reading Time.

Answer the Part A Questions. Answer the 10 questions that follow the selection. There are 5 fact questions and 5 thought questions. Choose the best answer to each question and put an X in that box.

Read the Part B Selection. This passage is less textbook-like and more story-like than the timed selection. Read well enough so that you can answer the questions that follow.

Answer the Part B Questions. These questions are different from traditional multiple-choice questions. In answering these questions, you must make three choices for each question. Instructions for answering each category of question are given. There are 15 responses for you to record.

Correct Your Answers. Use the Answer Key at the back of the book. For the Part A questions, circle any wrong answer and put an X in the box you should have marked. For the Part B questions, circle any wrong answer and write the correct letter or number next to it.

Scoring Your Work

Total Your Correct Answers. Count your correct answers for Part A and for Part B. Record those numbers on the appropriate lines at the end of the lesson. Then add the two scores to determine your total correct answers. Record that number on the appropriate line.

Plotting Your Progress

Plot Your Reading Time. Refer to the Reading Rate graph on page 116. On the vertical line that represents your lesson, put an X at the point where it intersects your reading time, shown along the left-hand side. The right-hand side of the graph will reveal your words-per-minute reading speed. Your instructor will review this graph from time to time to evaluate your progress.

Plot Your Comprehension Scores. Record your comprehension scores on the graph on page 117. On the vertical line that represents your lesson, put an X at the point where it intersects your total correct answers, shown along the left-hand side. The right-hand side of the graph will reveal your comprehension percentage. Your instructor will want to review this graph, too. Your achievement, as shown on both graphs, will determine your readiness to move on to higher and more challenging levels.

Plot Your Comprehension Skills. You will find the Comprehension Skills Profile on page 118. It is used to record your wrong answers only for the Part B questions. The five categories of questions are listed along the bottom. There are five columns of boxes, one column for each question. For every wrong answer, put an X in a box for that question. Your instructor will use this graph to detect any comprehension problems you may be experiencing.

PART A: READING FASTER AND BETTER

Step 1: Preview

When you read, do you start in with the first word, or do you look over the whole selection for a moment? Good readers preview the selection first. This helps make them good—and fast—readers. Here are the steps to follow when previewing the timed selection in Part A of each unit.

1. Read the Title. Titles are designed not only to announce the subject, but also to make the reader think. What can you learn from the title? What thoughts does it bring to mind? What do you already know about this subject?

2. Read the First Sentence. Read the first two sentences if they are short. The opening sentence is the writer's opportunity to greet the reader. Some writers announce what they hope to tell you in the selection. Some writers tell you why they are writing. Other writers just try to get your attention.

3. Read the Last Sentence. Read the final two sentences if they are short. The closing sentence is the writer's last chance to talk to you. Some writers repeat the main idea once more. Some writers draw a conclusion—this is what they have been leading up to. Other writers summarize their thoughts; they tie all the facts together.

4. Scan the Selection. Glance through the selection quickly to see what else you can pick up. Look for anything that can help you read the selection. Are there names, dates, or numbers? If so, you may have to read more slowly. Is the selection informative—containing a lot of facts, or is it conversational—an informal discussion with the reader?

Step 2: Read for Meaning

When you read, do you just see words? Are you so occupied reading words that you sometimes fail to get the meaning? Good readers see beyond the words—they seek the meaning. This makes them faster readers.

1. Build Concentration. You cannot read with understanding if you are not concentrating. When you discover that your thoughts are straying, correct the situation right away. Avoid distractions and distracting situations. Keep the preview information in mind. This will help focus your attention on the selection.

2. Read in Thought Groups. A reader should strive to see words in meaningful combinations. If you see only a word at a time (called word-by-word reading), your comprehension suffers along with your speed.

3. Question the Writer. To sustain the pace you have set for yourself, and to maintain a high level of concentration and comprehension, question the writer as you read. Ask yourself such questions as, "What does this mean? How can I use this information?"

Step 3: Grasp Paragraph Sense

The paragraph is the basic unit of meaning. If you can discover quickly and understand the main point of each paragraph, you can comprehend the writer's message. Good readers know how to find the main ideas quickly. This helps make them faster readers.

1. Find the Topic Sentence. The topic sentence, which contains the main idea, is often the first sentence of a paragraph. It is followed by sentences that support, develop, or explain the main idea. Sometimes a topic sentence comes at the end of a paragraph. When it does, the supporting details come first, building the base for the topic sentence. Some paragraphs do not have a topic sentence; all of the sentences combine to create a meaningful idea.

2. Understand Paragraph Structure. Every well-written paragraph has a purpose. The purpose may be to inform, define, explain, illustrate, and so on. The purpose should always relate to the main idea and expand on it. As you read each paragraph, see how the body of the paragraph is used to tell you more about the main idea.

Step 4: Organize Facts

When you read, do you tend to see a lot of facts without any apparent connection or relationship? Understanding how the facts all fit together to deliver the writer's message is, after all, the reason for reading. Good readers organize facts as they read. This helps them read rapidly and well.

1. Discover the Writer's Plan. Every writer has a plan or outline to follow. If you can discover the writer's method of organization, you have a key to understanding the message. Sometimes the writer gives you obvious signals. The statement, "There are three reasons . . .," should prompt you to look for a listing of the three items. Other less obvious signal words such as *moreover, otherwise,* and *consequently* tell you the direction the writer is taking in delivering a message.

2. Relate as You Read. As you read the selection, keep the information learned during the preview in mind. See how the writer is attempting to piece together a meaningful message. As you discover the relationship among the ideas, the message comes through quickly and clearly.

PART B: MASTERING READING COMPREHENSION

Recognizing Words in Context

Always check to see if the words around a new word—its context—can give you some clue to its meaning. A word generally appears in a context related to its meaning. If the words *soil* and *seeds* appear in an article about gardens, for example, you can assume they are related to the topic of gardens.

Suppose you are unsure of the meaning of the word *expired* in the following paragraph:

> Vera wanted to take a book out, but her library card had expired. She had to borrow mine because she didn't have time to renew hers.

You could begin to figure out the meaning of *expired* by asking yourself, "What could have happened to Vera's library card that would make her have to borrow someone else's card?" You might realize that if she had to renew her card, it must have come to an end or run out. This would lead you to conclude that the word *expired* must mean to come to an end or run out. You would be right. The context suggested the meaning to you.

Context can also affect the meaning of a word you know. The word *key,* for instance, has many meanings. There are musical keys, door keys, and keys to solving a mystery. The context in which *key* occurs will tell you which meaning is right.

Sometimes a hard word will be explained by the words that immediately follow it. The word *grave* in the following sentence might give you trouble:

> He looked grave; there wasn't a trace of a smile on his lips.

You can figure out that the second part of the sentence explains the word *grave:* "wasn't a trace of a smile" indicates a serious look, so *grave* must mean serious.

The subject of a sentence and your knowledge about that subject might also help you determine the meaning of an unknown word. Try to decide the meaning of the word *revive* in the following sentence:

> Sunshine and water will revive those drooping plants.

The sentence is about giving plants light and water. You may know that plants need light and water to be healthy. If you know that drooping plants are not healthy, you can figure out that *revive* means to bring back to health.

Distinguishing Fact from Opinion

Every day you are called upon to sort out fact and opinion. When a friend says she saw Mel Gibson's greatest movie last night, she is giving you her opinion. When she says she saw Mel Gibson's latest movie, she may be stating a fact. The fact can be proved—you can check to confirm or verify that the movie is indeed Mel Gibson's most recent film. The opinion can be disputed—ask around and others may not agree about the film's unqualified greatness. Because much of what you read and hear contains both facts and opinions, you need to be able to tell them apart. You need the skill of distinguishing fact from opinion.

Facts are statements that can be proved true. The proof must be objective and verifiable. You must be able to check for yourself to confirm a fact.

Look at the following facts. Notice that they can be checked for accuracy and confirmed. Suggested sources for verification appear in parentheses.

- In 1998 Bill Clinton was president of the United States. (Consult newspapers, news broadcasts, election results, etc.)

- Earth revolves around the sun. (Look it up in encyclopedias or astrological journals; ask knowledgeable people.)

- Dogs walk on four legs. (See for yourself.)

Opinions are statements that cannot be proved true. There is no objective evidence you can consult to check the truthfulness of an opinion. Unlike facts, opinions express personal beliefs or judgments. Opinions reveal how someone feels about a subject, not the facts about that subject. You might agree or disagree with someone's opinion, but you cannot prove it right or wrong.

Look at the following opinions. Reasons for classification as opinions appear in parentheses.

- Bill Clinton was born to be a president. (You cannot prove this by referring to birth records. There is no evidence to support this belief.)

- Intelligent life exists on other planets in our solar system. (There is no proof of this. It may be proved true some day, but for now it is just an educated guess—not a fact.)

- Dog is man's best friend. (This is not a fact; your best friend might not be a dog.)

As you read, be aware that facts and opinions are frequently mixed together. The following passage contains both facts and opinions:

> The new 2000 Cruising Yacht offers lots of real-life interior room. It features a luxurious aft cabin, not some dim "cave." The galley

comes equipped with a full-size refrigerator and freezer. And this spacious galley has room to spare. The heads (there are two) have separate showers. The fit and finish are beyond equal and the performance is responsive and outstanding.

Did you detect that the third and fifth sentences state facts and that the rest of the sentences express opinions? Both facts and opinions are useful to you as a reader. But to evaluate what you read and to read intelligently, you need to know the difference between them.

Keeping Events in Order

Writers organize details in a pattern. They present information in a certain order. Recognizing how writers organize—and understanding that organization—can help you improve your comprehension.

When details are arranged in the precise order in which they occurred, a writer is using a chronological (or time) pattern. A writer may, however, change this order. The story may "flash back" to past events that affected the present. The story may "flash forward" to show the results of present events. The writer may move back and forth between past, present, and future to help you see the importance of events.

Making Correct Inferences

Much of what you read suggests more than it says. Writers do not always state outright what they want you to know. Frequently, they omit information that underlies the statements they make. They may assume that you already know it. They may want you to make the effort to figure out the implied information. To get the most out of what you read, you must come to an understanding about unstated information. You can do this through inference. From what is stated, you make inferences about what is not.

You make many inferences every day. Imagine, for example, that you are visiting a friend's house for the first time. You see a bag of dog food. You infer (make an inference) that the family has a dog. On another day you overhear a conversation. You catch the names of two actors and the words *scene, dialogue,* and *directing.* You infer that the people are discussing a movie or play.

In these situations and others like them, you infer unstated information from what you observe or read. Readers who cannot make inferences cannot see beyond the obvious. For the careful reader, facts are just the beginning. Facts stimulate your mind to think beyond them—to make an inference about what is meant but not stated.

The following passage is about Charles Dickens. As you read it, see how many inferences you can make.

Charles Dickens visited the United States in 1867. Wherever he went, the reception was the same. The night before, crowds arrived and lined up before the door. By morning the streets were campgrounds, with men, women, and children sitting or sleeping on blankets. Hustlers got ten times the price of a ticket. Once inside, audiences were surprised to hear their favorite Dickens characters speak with an English accent. After 76 readings Dickens boarded a ship for England. When his fellow passengers asked him to read, he said he'd rather be put in irons!

Did you notice that many inferences may be drawn from the passage? Dickens attracted huge crowds. From that fact you can infer that he was popular. His English accent surprised audiences. You can infer that many people didn't know he was English. Hustlers got high prices for tickets. This suggests that "scalping" tickets is not new. Dickens refused to read on the ship. You can infer that he was exhausted and tired of reading aloud to audiences. Those are some obvious inferences that can be made from the passage. More subtle ones can also be made; however, if you see the obvious ones, you understand how inferences are made.

Be careful about the inferences you make. One set of facts may suggest several inferences. Not all of them will be correct; some will be faulty inferences. The correct inference is supported by enough evidence to make it more likely than other inferences.

Understanding Main Ideas

The main idea tells who or what is the subject of the paragraph or passage. The main idea is the most important idea, the idea that provides purpose and direction. The rest of the paragraph or passage explains, develops, or supports the main idea. Without a main idea, there would be only a collection of unconnected thoughts. It would be like a handle and a bowl without the "idea cup," or bread and meat without the "idea sandwich."

In the following passage, the main idea is printed in italics. As you read, observe how the other sentences develop or explain the main idea.

Typhoon Chris hit with full fury today on the central coast of Japan. Heavy rain from the storm flooded the area. High waves carried many homes into the sea. People now fear that the heavy rains will cause mudslides in the central part of the country. The number of people killed by the storm may climb past the 200 mark by Saturday.

In this paragraph, the main idea statement appears first. It is followed by sentences that explain, support, or give details. Sometimes the main idea appears at the end of a paragraph. Writers often construct that type of paragraph when their purpose is to persuade or convince. Readers may be more open to a new idea if the reasons for it are presented first. As you read the following paragraph, think about the overall impact of the supporting ideas. Their purpose is to convince the reader that the main idea in the last sentence should be accepted.

Last week there was a head-on collision at Huntington and Canton streets. Just a month ago a pedestrian was struck there. Fortunately, she was only slightly injured. In the past year there have been more accidents there than at any other corner in the city. In fact, nearly 10 percent of all city accidents occur there. This intersection is dangerous, and a traffic signal should be installed there before a life is lost.

The details in the paragraph progress from least important to most important. They achieve their full effect in the main idea statement at the end.

In many cases, the main idea is not expressed in a single sentence. The reader is called upon to interpret all of the ideas expressed and decide upon a main idea. Read the following paragraph:

The American author Jack London was once a pupil at the Cole Grammar School in Oakland, California. Each morning the class sang a song. When the teacher noticed that Jack wouldn't sing, she sent him to the principal. He returned to class with a note. It said that he could be excused from singing if he would write an essay every morning.

In this paragraph, the reader has to interpret the individual ideas and decide on a main idea. This main idea seems reasonable: Jack London's career as a writer began with a "punishment" in grammar school.

Understanding the concept of the main idea and knowing how to find it is important. Transferring that understanding to your reading and study is also important.

1 A Lobsters

More than 30,000 known species of animals are included in the group known as crustaceans. Crustaceans are animals covered by hard shells, called exoskeletons. The exoskeleton is jointed at many points to permit movement. Crustaceans also have two pairs of antennae. The best-known crustaceans are lobsters, crabs, shrimp, and crayfish. Crustaceans occupy diverse environments throughout the world. Most live in marine habitats, but many inhabit freshwater or brackish areas, and others live on land.

Lobsters are found in all of the major seas. Because of their commercial importance, American lobsters are the best known. They live along the Atlantic coast from North Carolina to Labrador. In warm weather, lobsters stay near shore. As winter approaches, they may move to depths of more than 200 feet (60 meters). Most lobsters caught by fishers weigh less than 2 pounds (0.9 kilogram), but giant specimens weighing more than 40 pounds (18 kilograms) are sometimes taken. Lobsters are blue-green, spotted with green-black. Their enlarged front pincers are marked with orange. When a lobster is cooked, its shell turns a bright red.

As in other crustaceans, the lobster's body and appendages are covered by jointed shells. The abdomen is enclosed by six overlapping plates. A fan-shaped tailpiece serves as a rudder and oar. The lobster can move forward, but its fastest motion is in reverse, an action caused by a flip of its tail. One pair of appendages is a pair of claws. The larger claw is used for crushing while the smaller one is used for seizing and tearing prey.

American lobsters have been a favorite food since colonial times. To capture them, a slatted box called a lobster pot is baited with dead fish. It is then weighted and lowered to the bottom. One end of the lobster pot has a funnel-shaped opening made of heavy netting. The funnel points inward, making it easy for the lobster to enter but difficult for it to leave. During peak seasons, lobster fishers remove the lobsters and rebait their pots daily.

The lobster-fishing areas of Canada, extending along the coast of Quebec and in the Gulf of St. Lawrence, are the greatest in the world. The chief lobster-fishing areas of the United States are along the coast of Maine. The lobster industry is tightly regulated by both countries to avoid overfishing. Spawning females are protected, and lobsters below a minimum size may not be taken.

Reading Time _____

Recalling Facts

1. Exoskeletons are
   - ❏ a. bony plates.
   - ❏ b. hard, jointed shells.
   - ❏ c. a type of crustacean.

2. Most crustaceans live
   - ❏ a. in fresh water.
   - ❏ b. in marine habitats.
   - ❏ c. on land.

3. American lobsters are the best known because of
   - ❏ a. their commercial importance.
   - ❏ b. where they are found.
   - ❏ c. their size.

4. Lobsters move fastest
   - ❏ a. from side to side.
   - ❏ b. when going forward.
   - ❏ c. in reverse.

5. The best lobster-fishing areas are found in
   - ❏ a. the United States.
   - ❏ b. Mexico.
   - ❏ c. Canada.

Understanding Ideas

6. It is likely that crustaceans have exterior skeletons in order to
   - ❏ a. protect their soft bodies.
   - ❏ b. make them easier to eat.
   - ❏ c. distinguish them from fish.

7. Lobsters can live in many different habitats, which shows their
   - ❏ a. sensitivity.
   - ❏ b. adaptability.
   - ❏ c. mobility.

8. The size of a lobster is probably a good indication of its
   - ❏ a. flavor.
   - ❏ b. habitat.
   - ❏ c. age.

9. Lobster was a favorite food in colonial times, which suggests that
   - ❏ a. the colonies traded with Canada.
   - ❏ b. lobsters were usually imported from England.
   - ❏ c. lobsters were plentiful along the New England coast.

10. Tight regulations in the lobster industry show a concern for the
    - ❏ a. price of lobsters.
    - ❏ b. future supply of lobsters.
    - ❏ c. location of lobsters.

Free the Lobster!

Tara stood in front of the lobster tank in Sam's Seafoods. Inside the tank, a gigantic lobster waved its antennae at her. A sign on the tank read "World's Biggest Lobster. Raffle Tickets $5."

"Oh, Mom!" Tara cried. "We have to win it!"

"What would you do with it, Tara?" her mother asked.

"I'd set it free," she answered.

On the day of the raffle drawing, Tara stood in a crowd of people. "And the winner is . . . ," the fish-market owner drew out the moment, ". . . number 357!"

"That's my number! It's mine!" shouted a man.

"And what will you do with this lobster, sir?" the owner asked.

"Invite twenty-five friends to a lobster feast," the man said.

"You can't do that!" cried Tara. Everyone was looking at her now. "You have to let it go. That lobster must be at least fifty years old. It deserves to go on living. Think of all the dangers it's survived in its long lifetime. Please don't end it for it."

"I give in," said the man. "We'll let it go."

The whole crowd followed Tara and the man to the pier. They cheered when the huge lobster was set free. It seemed to wave a giant claw in farewell before it disappeared beneath the waves.

1. **Recognizing Words in Context**

Find the word *cried* in the passage. One definition below is a *synonym* for that word; it means the same or almost the same thing. One definition is an *antonym*; it has the opposite or nearly opposite meaning. The other has a completely different meaning. Label the definitions S for *synonym*, A for *antonym*, and D for *different*.

_____ a. shouted

_____ b. whispered

_____ c. wept

2. **Distinguishing Fact from Opinion**

Two of the statements below present *facts*, which can be proved correct. The other statement is an *opinion*, which expresses someone's thoughts or beliefs. Label the statements F for *fact* and O for *opinion*.

_____ a. The lobster had lived for a long time.

_____ b. Tara wanted to set the lobster free.

_____ c. The lobster deserved to go on living.

3. Keeping Events in Order

Two of the statements below describe events that happened at the same time. The other statement describes an event that happened before or after those events. Label them S for *same time*, B for *before*, and A for *after*.

_____ a. Tara and the man set the lobster free.

_____ b. The watching crowd cheered.

_____ c. A man had the winning raffle ticket.

4. Making Correct Inferences

Two of the statements below are correct *inferences*, or reasonable guesses. They are based on information in the passage. The other statement is an incorrect, or faulty, inference. Label the statements C for *correct* inference and F for *faulty* inference.

_____ a. Tara and her mother bought a raffle ticket for the lobster.

_____ b. Tara never ate lobster meat.

_____ c. The larger a lobster is, the older it is.

5. Understanding Main Ideas

One of the statements below expresses the main idea of the passage. One statement is too general, or too broad. The other explains only part of the passage; it is too narrow. Label the statements M for *main idea*, B for *too broad*, and N for *too narrow*.

_____ a. Tara wanted to win a lobster in order to set it free.

_____ b. A giant lobster was being raffled off.

_____ c. Over its lifetime, a lobster faces many dangers.

Correct Answers, Part A _____

Correct Answers, Part B _____

Total Correct Answers _____

2   A   Down on the Farm

Humans began to form permanent settlements. They gave up wandering in search of food. Thus, agriculture was born. From the beginning, agriculture has included raising both crops and livestock. At first, this new way of providing food and other raw materials developed slowly. It made life much easier for many people. Agriculture became the preferred way of supplying a basic human need. The people who worked at agriculture came to be called farmers.

Society was different before there were farmers. Some people devoted time to gathering plants for food. Others went hunting or fishing. When food was abundant, there were feasts. When it was not, there was famine. Gradually, people discovered the advantages of caring for animals in flocks and herds. They learned to grow plants for food, medicine, clothing, and shelter.

The food supply became more reliable. Raw materials became more abundant. Some people were free to do other things besides farming and hunting. Many of them chose to live in towns and cities. Here, using their talents in various ways, they became expert in different trades. They made a variety of goods. They could trade their goods with the farmers for food. Other people used their new free time to observe, to think, and to learn. As centuries passed, such activity led to the bases of science, religion, government, and the arts. These are the foundation of modern civilization.

Farming used to be primarily a family enterprise. To a large extent, it still is in most countries. In the more developed areas, however, efficient large-scale operations are overtaking smaller family farms. These large farms usually specialize in one type of crop. The farms are often run by giant parent corporations. Such farms are part of the current trend toward more controlled and cost-effective agriculture. The new business is called agribusiness.

The goals in agriculture have almost always been increased production and decreased labor. In the early 1900s, the American farm was run by the muscles of people and animals. Today there are machines of great size and complexity. Some are computerized. Machines can accomplish in hours what took people and animals days to do. There are still family farms, but they are becoming fewer every year. There are also small-scale agricultural systems in many emerging nations of the world. But the trend is toward larger farms. Mechanized farms use the latest scientific methods to provide products more efficiently.

Reading Time _____

Recalling Facts

1. Agriculture was the result of
   - ❑ a. famine.
   - ❑ b. a lack of wild animals.
   - ❑ c. humans forming permanent settlements.

2. Besides growing crops, agriculture involves
   - ❑ a. hunting.
   - ❑ b. raising livestock.
   - ❑ c. building houses.

3. In developed areas, farming is primarily
   - ❑ a. a family enterprise.
   - ❑ b. a large-scale business.
   - ❑ c. run by muscle power.

4. The goals in agriculture are
   - ❑ a. increased production and increased labor.
   - ❑ b. decreased production and decreased labor.
   - ❑ c. increased production and decreased labor.

5. The trend in agriculture is toward
   - ❑ a. small-scale agricultural systems.
   - ❑ b. larger, mechanized farms.
   - ❑ c. larger, family-run farms.

Understanding Ideas

6. An advantage of farming over hunting was
   - ❑ a. a more consistent food supply.
   - ❑ b. both men and women could farm.
   - ❑ c. farming eliminated famine.

7. Agriculture helped advance modern civilization by
   - ❑ a. providing people with more spare time.
   - ❑ b. creating jobs for more people.
   - ❑ c. attracting people to the country.

8. Cost-effective agriculture means
   - ❑ a. crops cost more to grow.
   - ❑ b. crops cost more to buy.
   - ❑ c. crops cost less to grow.

9. Greater efficiency in agriculture means replacing
   - ❑ a. products with computers.
   - ❑ b. farms with corporations.
   - ❑ c. people and animals with machines.

10. It is likely that as countries become more developed,
    - ❑ a. each country will specialize in one type of crop.
    - ❑ b. family farms will become fewer.
    - ❑ c. more people will become farmers.

Mina stooped low over the berry bushes, her fingers seeking the last few berries. Tiny as they were, the berries tasted better than the roots and tree bark she had been eating lately.

She stood up and started back to the camp. Soon her people would be moving on. The men had had no luck hunting. The women and children had searched for edible plants, berries, nuts, and seeds, but there was little left to find. When food became scarce, the people wandered on to somewhere else.

A short time ago, the people had camped on a plain where the tall grass seemed to go on forever. The women and children had gathered the fat grass seeds, filling their baskets to overflowing. Roasted over a fire, the seeds tasted good. But the season of grass had passed and the people moved on. "I wish I had brought some of those seeds with me," Mina thought now.

Once Mina had spilled some grass seeds on the ground. A few days later, she saw new grass growing in that spot where no grass had grown before. A thought came to Mina. If the people could grow their own plants, they wouldn't have to keep wandering. "Someday I'm going to put some seeds in the ground and see if they grow," Mina said to herself.

1. Recognizing Words in Context

Find the word *short* in the passage. One definition below is a *synonym* for that word; it means the same or almost the same thing. One definition is an *antonym*; it has the opposite or nearly opposite meaning. The other has a completely different meaning. Label the definitions S for *synonym*, A for *antonym*, and D for *different*.

_____ a. low

_____ b. long

_____ c. brief

2. Distinguishing Fact from Opinion

Two of the statements below present *facts*, which can be proved correct. The other statement is an *opinion*, which expresses someone's thoughts or beliefs. Label the statements F for *fact* and O for *opinion*.

_____ a. Mina was the smartest person in the group.

_____ b. Mina's people ate plants, berries, nuts, and seeds.

_____ c. When food was scarce, Mina's people moved on.

3. Keeping Events in Order

Label the statements below 1, 2, and 3 to show the order in which the events happened.

_____ a. Mina gathered some berries.

_____ b. Mina spilled grass seeds onto the ground.

_____ c. Grass grew where Mina spilled grass seeds.

4. Making Correct Inferences

Two of the statements below are correct *inferences*, or reasonable guesses. They are based on information in the passage. The other statement is an incorrect, or faulty, inference. Label the statements C for *correct* inference and F for *faulty* inference.

_____ a. Mina made a connection between the spilled seeds and the new grass that grew.

_____ b. The people were not smart enough to grow their own food.

_____ c. Among Mina's people, men and women had different roles when it came to providing food.

5. Understanding Main Ideas

One of the statements below expresses the main idea of the passage. One statement is too general, or too broad. The other explains only part of the passage; it is too narrow. Label the statements M for *main idea*, B for *too broad*, and N for *too narrow*.

_____ a. Mina spilled some grass seeds on the ground.

_____ b. Agriculture was born when hunter-gatherers gave up wandering in search of food and formed permanent settlements.

_____ c. Mina had an idea about growing food that would change the way of life of her people.

Correct Answers, Part A _____

Correct Answers, Part B _____

Total Correct Answers _____

Once called a genius without judgment, Sir Winston Churchill rose through a stormy career to become a respected political leader during World War II. He was one of Britain's greatest prime ministers.

Winston Churchill was born on November 30, 1874, at Blenheim Palace. His father was Lord Randolph Churchill, the third son of the seventh duke. His mother, Jennie Jerome, had been a New York society beauty. As Winston grew to boyhood, his grandfather became viceroy of Ireland and his father served as viceregal secretary. So Winston spent his early years in Dublin, then attended two private schools in England.

When he was 12, his father sent him to Harrow. A chunky explosive redhead, Winston stayed in the lowest grades longer than anyone else. In later life he said, "Being so long in the lowest grades I gained an immense advantage over the clever boys. They all went on to learn Latin and Greek and splendid things like that. But I was taught English. Thus I got into my bones the structure of the ordinary English sentence which is a noble thing." When he was 16, he entered Sandhurst, an historic British military college. There he excelled in studies of tactics and fortifications and graduated eighth in a class of 150.

In March 1895, he became a sublieutenant in a distinguished cavalry regiment. He also began to write. From reading great works, he learned his skills as an orator. He joined an infantry regiment in India in 1897. In 1898, he joined the British Army in the Sudan. Following the battle of Khartoum, he was decorated for bravery.

Churchill's return to England in 1899 changed his career. Disliking his low army salary, he determined to enter politics. But when he ran for Parliament, he was defeated. Churchill was undaunted.

At the outbreak of the Boer War in South Africa in 1899, he obtained an assignment from the *Morning Post* as war correspondent. Churchill rode into the thick of the battles. In one engagement, he was captured and imprisoned, along with captured officers, in a school building. He made a bold escape and eventually reached the British lines, some 300 miles (483 kilometers) away.

Upon his return to England, Churchill made up for an old defeat, as he was to do so often in his life. The same voters who had rejected him earlier now elected him to Parliament as a hero.

Reading Time _____

Recalling Facts

1. Winston Churchill was one of Great Britain's greatest
   - ❑ a. presidents.
   - ❑ b. teachers.
   - ❑ c. prime ministers.

2. Churchill left the army because
   - ❑ a. he was tired of fighting wars.
   - ❑ b. of his low army salary.
   - ❑ c. he wanted to be a writer.

3. Churchill was defeated
   - ❑ a. at the battle of Khartoum.
   - ❑ b. when he first ran for Parliament.
   - ❑ c. by poor health.

4. Churchill was captured and imprisoned while serving
   - ❑ a. as a military doctor.
   - ❑ b. in the infantry.
   - ❑ c. as a war correspondent.

5. After the Boer War, Churchill
   - ❑ a. became a member of Parliament.
   - ❑ b. turned to writing.
   - ❑ c. retired.

Understanding Ideas

6. You can conclude from the article that Winston Churchill's mother, Jennie Jerome, was
   - ❑ a. French.
   - ❑ b. American.
   - ❑ c. English.

7. As a young boy, Churchill was
   - ❑ a. a poor student.
   - ❑ b. disobedient.
   - ❑ c. good at sports.

8. Churchill considered the study of English
   - ❑ a. boring.
   - ❑ b. useless.
   - ❑ c. valuable.

9. The British people admired Churchill for his
   - ❑ a. noble background.
   - ❑ b. military skills.
   - ❑ c. ability to change careers.

10. Calling Churchill a genius without judgment meant that Churchill
    - ❑ a. lacked common sense.
    - ❑ b. was too smart.
    - ❑ c. was cowardly.

Winston Churchill's School Days

Like most boys of his time from wealthy families, Winston Churchill was sent to boarding school at the age of seven. His parents deposited him, already homesick and thoroughly miserable, at the school one dark November evening.

Having missed part of the term, Winston had to catch up. He was taken to the Latin teacher, who gave him a paper with six forms of the Latin noun *mensa* to memorize. The words had no meaning for him, but Winston memorized them anyway. The teacher came back and was pleased that Winston could recite the forms of the noun perfectly.

Then Winston made his first big mistake. "What does it mean?" he asked. The teacher explained that *mensa* meant "table." But why, Winston wanted to know, did it also mean "O table"? Somewhat impatiently, the teacher explained that this was the form of the word one used when one wanted to speak to a table.

"But I never do!" Churchill responded.

Annoyed, the teacher told him that such impertinence would be punished severely. So in his first hours at school, Churchill had already begun to gain a reputation for being both too smart for his own good and too stubborn to learn.

1. **Recognizing Words in Context**

   Find the word *impertinence* in the passage. One definition below is a *synonym* for that word; it means the same or almost the same thing. One definition is an *antonym;* it has the opposite or nearly opposite meaning. The other has a completely different meaning. Label the definitions S for *synonym,* A for *antonym,* and D for *different.*

   _____ a. courtesy

   _____ b. disrespect

   _____ c. laziness

2. **Distinguishing Fact from Opinion**

   Two of the statements below present *facts,* which can be proved correct. The other statement is an *opinion,* which expresses someone's thoughts or beliefs. Label the statements F for *fact* and O for *opinion.*

   _____ a. Winston Churchill was sent to boarding school at the age of seven.

   _____ b. Churchill memorized the six forms of the noun *mensa.*

   _____ c. Asking a question was Churchill's first big mistake.

3. Keeping Events in Order

Label the statements below 1, 2, and 3 to show the order in which the events happened.

_____ a. Churchill's parents took him to boarding school.

_____ b. Churchill was given the forms of the noun *mensa* to memorize.

_____ c. The Latin teacher told Winston he would be punished.

4. Making Correct Inferences

Two of the statements below are correct *inferences,* or reasonable guesses. They are based on information in the passage. The other statement is an incorrect, or faulty, inference. Label the statements C for *correct* inference and F for *faulty* inference.

_____ a. Churchill's school did not encourage independent thinking.

_____ b. As a child, Churchill was deliberately rude.

_____ c. Curiosity about the reasons for things was one of Churchill's characteristics.

5. Understanding Main Ideas

One of the statements below expresses the main idea of the passage. One statement is too general, or too broad. The other explains only part of the passage; it is too narrow. Label the statements M for *main idea,* B for *too broad,* and N for *too narrow.*

_____ a. Boarding schools can be terrible places.

_____ b. One of the six forms of the Latin word *mensa* that Churchill had to memorize means "O table."

_____ c. Churchill's lively intelligence got him started on the wrong foot at his first boarding school.

Correct Answers, Part A _____

Correct Answers, Part B _____

Total Correct Answers _____

Weapons of War

Not all weapons have been invented solely for the purpose of war. Despite humans' war-filled past, there is much evidence that the ordinary person does not like to kill or be killed, to maim or be maimed, to plunder or be plundered. Certainly, humankind's first desire is to continue to live, to preserve self and family. For this purpose, humans first used a club—to kill an animal for food. Later, they learned that the same club could kill a person, too.

The club was an effective war weapon, even if it had been borrowed from civilian life. With a rock fastened to the end of the stout stick, it became even more efficient in smashing an opponent's skull. When the rock was chipped so as to present a sharpened edge, its destructive qualities were further increased.

So universal was the use of the club that it may be considered the ancestor of all other war weapons. Many ways have been found to improve it. A long shaft with a metal head can be deadly in strong hands, but even deadlier when a series of loose metal rings is placed around the shaft. As the attacker swings the club, the metal rings slide up to the end, adding their speed and weight to the metal head just as it strikes the victim.

Symbols of the club remain even in modern warfare. The field marshal's baton and the emperor's scepter are insignia of power—the power of the one who wields a club.

The club was the principal weapon of war. However, it did not remain a mere club for long. In the Stone Age, it became the stone ax with a sharpened edge. When iron was first smelted, it was used to make even stronger and sharper war clubs. In time, spikes were added to the sharp edges to make a battle-ax that would kill by one of three methods, no matter what the angle of attack—crushing, cutting, or perforating.

The discovery of metals—first copper, then bronze and iron—made possible sharper and stronger weapons. Daggers and knives took on thousands of different shapes. The dagger and knife were small weapons, but the development of the sword added several feet of striking power to an attacker's arm. Throughout the world, there can be found as many shapes and sizes of swords as human ingenuity could conceive and manufacture.

Reading Time _____

Recalling Facts

1. Humans' first use of a club was probably to
   - ❏ a. kill an animal for food.
   - ❏ b. kill an animal for sport.
   - ❏ c. kill another person.

2. Loose metal rings placed around the shaft make a club
   - ❏ a. swing slower.
   - ❏ b. swing faster.
   - ❏ c. less accurate.

3. A battle-ax with spikes could kill by
   - ❏ a. swinging, stabbing, or attacking.
   - ❏ b. crushing, cutting, or perforating.
   - ❏ c. sharpening, smashing, or striking.

4. Sharper and stronger weapons were made possible by the discovery of
   - ❏ a. how to sharpen edges.
   - ❏ b. metals.
   - ❏ c. stone.

5. A weapon that adds several feet of striking power to an attacker's arm is the
   - ❏ a. dagger.
   - ❏ b. knife.
   - ❏ c. sword.

Understanding Ideas

6. According to the article, all humans have the desire for
   - ❏ a. improvement.
   - ❏ b. self-preservation.
   - ❏ c. destruction.

7. You can conclude from the article that most weapons were invented
   - ❏ a. for use in war.
   - ❏ b. for self-protection.
   - ❏ c. to acquire food.

8. Over time, weapons became
   - ❏ a. less dangerous.
   - ❏ b. heavier.
   - ❏ c. more destructive.

9. It is likely that weapons such as daggers and knives are most useful
   - ❏ a. in close combat.
   - ❏ b. when fighting from a distance.
   - ❏ c. for hunting.

10. The article suggests that today, symbols of warfare are regarded with
    - ❏ a. dislike.
    - ❏ b. respect.
    - ❏ c. indifference.

Stone Age Weapons

The Neanderthal toolmaker chose a stone. One of a long line of toolmakers, he knew which stones were best. This stone was especially desirable—it was flint. By striking the stone in the correct way, he could make it break as he chose.

Tribe members watched in awe as the toolmaker struck the flint with his striking stone to expose its solid central core. He examined the piece of flint closely and decided it would make a good hand ax.

The toolmaker struck the flint with his hammer. With each blow, large, sharp chips fell away until the flint had the rough shape of a hand ax. Now he chose another tool, a bone hammer, to shape the edges of the ax. Smaller pieces fell away, making the edges of the ax thin and sharp.

The toolmaker examined the new ax. About five inches (12.7 centimeters) long, with sharp edges on either side, it could be used to chop wood, kill a large animal, or butcher meat. The chips that had fallen from its sides would make smaller weapons—knives and spearheads. In an age when tools and weapons were the same, these were the basic tools of Neanderthal existence.

1. Recognizing Words in Context

Find the word *blow* in the passage. One definition below is a *synonym* for that word; it means the same or almost the same thing. One definition is an *antonym;* it has the opposite or nearly opposite meaning. The other has a completely different meaning. Label the definitions S for *synonym,* A for *antonym,* and D for *different.*

_____ a. send forth air

_____ b. caress

_____ c. hit

2. Distinguishing Fact from Opinion

Two of the statements below present *facts,* which can be proved correct. The other statement is an *opinion,* which expresses someone's thoughts or beliefs. Label the statements F for *fact* and O for *opinion.*

_____ a. The toolmaker shaped the flint by striking it with a stone hammer.

_____ b. The hand ax was about five inches (12.7 centimeters) long.

_____ c. Flint was the most desirable stone of all.

3. Keeping Events in Order

Two of the statements below describe events that happened at the same time. The other statement describes an event that happened before or after those events. Label them S for *same time*, B for *before*, and A for *after*.

_____ a. Tribe members watched in awe.

_____ b. The toolmaker chose a piece of flint.

_____ c. The toolmaker struck the flint with his striking stone.

4. Making Correct Inferences

Two of the statements below are correct *inferences*, or reasonable guesses. They are based on information in the passage. The other statement is an incorrect, or faulty, inference. Label the statements C for *correct* inference and F for *faulty* inference.

_____ a. Neanderthal toolmakers were skilled craftspeople.

_____ b. Neanderthal toolmakers were highly respected in their tribes.

_____ c. Without flint, the Neanderthals would have had no tools.

5. Understanding Main Ideas

One of the statements below expresses the main idea of the passage. One statement is too general, or too broad. The other explains only part of the passage; it is too narrow. Label the statements M for *main idea*, B for *too broad*, and N for *too narrow*.

_____ a. Neanderthal toolmakers skillfully crafted tools by striking flint to create axes, knives, and spearheads.

_____ b. One of the chief skills of the Neanderthals was toolmaking.

_____ c. The stone hand ax could be used to chop wood, kill a large animal, or butcher meat.

Correct Answers, Part A _____

Correct Answers, Part B _____

Total Correct Answers _____

Leif the Lucky

The first European to land on the North American continent was a Viking, Leif Ericson. Son of the explorer Eric the Red, Leif was born in Iceland in about A.D. 980. When Leif was about 2 years old, Eric took his family to Greenland. The boy grew up in Brattahild, now the village of Kagsiarsuk, on the southwest coast.

At 19, Leif voyaged to Norway, where he spent a winter at the court of Norway's Christian king. When he returned home, he converted his mother to Christianity. She built the first church in Greenland; its foundations and those of other Viking buildings may be seen in Kagsiarsuk.

There are different versions of how Leif discovered America. According to the "Saga of Eric," he was blown off his course on his return from Norway and was carried westward to the continent. Another saga says that in 985 Bjarni Herjulfsson saw land—probably the coast of North America—but did not go ashore. Years later, in Greenland, Leif bought a ship from Bjarni, gathered a crew of 35, and set off for the unknown land. They put ashore at a place described as a barren tableland of flat rocks backed by great ice mountains.

Going to sea again, the Vikings dropped anchor off a level, wooded land with broad stretches of white sand, which they called Markland (Forest Land). Once again they sailed southward. This time they went ashore where the land was green with self-sown wheat, trees, and sweet wild grapes. They named the place Vinland and here they built shelters and spent the winter.

Historians believe that Leif landed somewhere on the northernmost tip of Newfoundland on the Strait of Belle Isle. The theory was confirmed in 1963 after a Norwegian expedition uncovered the remains of a Viking settlement near the fishing village. Radiocarbon dating of charcoal found in hearths shows the site was used in about A.D. 1000. Two early fifteenth-century books also confirm the Vikings' settlement.

Leif earned his nickname Leif the Lucky on his trip home to Greenland, when he rescued a shipwrecked party of 15.

Thorfinn Karlsefni, an Icelander, established a colony in Vinland. This colony of 160 men and five women spent three years at Leif's wintering place. Karlsefni's son Snorri was the first child of European descent born in North America. The remains found by the Norwegian expedition may be those of Karlsefni's colony.

Reading Time _____

Recalling Facts

1. Leif Ericson was the first
   - ❏ a. North American to land in Newfoundland.
   - ❏ b. Viking to sail across the Atlantic Ocean.
   - ❏ c. European to land on the North American continent.

2. Leif Ericson was born in
   - ❏ a. Greenland.
   - ❏ b. Iceland.
   - ❏ c. Norway.

3. Historians believe that Leif landed
   - ❏ a. on the northernmost tip of Newfoundland.
   - ❏ b. on the southernmost tip of Newfoundland.
   - ❏ c. on an island off the North Atlantic coast.

4. The date of an early Vinland settlement was determined by radiocarbon dating of
   - ❏ a. wood used to build huts.
   - ❏ b. human bones.
   - ❏ c. charcoal found in hearths.

5. Leif earned his nickname Leif the Lucky when he
   - ❏ a. returned to Greenland.
   - ❏ b. rescued a shipwrecked party.
   - ❏ c. survived a hurricane.

Understanding Ideas

6. A good word to describe Leif Ericson is
   - ❏ a. timid.
   - ❏ b. foolhardy.
   - ❏ c. adventurous.

7. You can conclude from the article that early explorers like Leif Ericson
   - ❏ a. led carefree lives.
   - ❏ b. risked their lives by sailing into uncharted territory.
   - ❏ c. knew what to expect when sailing from their home countries.

8. Before radiocarbon dating, scientists had
   - ❏ a. incorrect theories about where Leif Ericson landed.
   - ❏ b. already proved where Leif Ericson landed.
   - ❏ c. no proof about where Leif Ericson landed.

9. Without proof, historians
   - ❏ a. have no idea when past events occurred.
   - ❏ b. can make educated guesses about when past events occurred.
   - ❏ c. should not draw any conclusions about when past events occurred.

10. The true story about Leif Ericson's discovery of America
    - ❏ a. will probably never be known.
    - ❏ b. will undoubtedly be discovered through radiocarbon dating.
    - ❏ c. is most likely different from the versions discussed in the article.

The Voyage of Bjarni Herjulfsson

As a young man in Iceland, Bjarni Herjulfsson loved seafaring. He acquired his own ship and goods to trade, and he made yearly trading trips to Norway.

One summer, when Bjarni returned to Iceland from Norway, he found that his father had sold his land and gone off to start a settlement in Greenland. Knowing that the new settlement would need his goods, Bjarni decided to sail on to Greenland.

Several days into the voyage, strong winds blew Bjarni's ship off course. Then heavy fog settled in, making it impossible to determine the ship's position by the stars. When the winds let up and the fog cleared, Bjarni found that he was far to the south of Greenland. He saw an unfamiliar land of low, wooded shores off to the west. This was definitely not the icy mountains of Greenland! Bjarni sailed northward, sighting land twice more, but he did not land to explore it.

In time, Bjarni reached Greenland, where he was welcomed by his father and the other settlers. That voyage was Bjarni's last. He settled down in Greenland to farm his father's land, never having set foot on the strange, new land he had seen to the west.

1. **Recognizing Words in Context**

   Find the word *strange* in the passage. One definition below is a *synonym* for that word; it means the same or almost the same thing. One definition is an *antonym;* it has the opposite or nearly opposite meaning. The other has a completely different meaning. Label the definitions S for *synonym*, A for *antonym*, and D for *different*.

   _____ a. unfamiliar

   _____ b. familiar

   _____ c. odd

2. **Distinguishing Fact from Opinion**

   Two of the statements below present *facts*, which can be proved correct. The other statement is an *opinion*, which expresses someone's thoughts or beliefs. Label the statements F for *fact* and O for *opinion*.

   _____ a. Bjarni sailed past the new land without going ashore.

   _____ b. Bjarni was foolish not to explore the new land.

   _____ c. Strong winds blew Bjarni's ship off course.

3. Keeping Events in Order

Two of the statements below describe events that happened at the same time. The other statement describes an event that happened before or after those events. Label them S for *same time*, B for *before*, and A for *after*.

_____ a. Bjarni's ship was blown far off course.

_____ b. The winds let up and the fog cleared.

_____ c. Bjarni found that he was far south of Greenland.

4. Making Correct Inferences

Two of the statements below are correct *inferences*, or reasonable guesses. They are based on information in the passage. The other statement is an incorrect, or faulty, inference. Label the statements C for *correct* inference and F for *faulty* inference.

_____ a. Bjarni was not interested in exploring the new lands.

_____ b. The new lands Bjarni saw were part of North America.

_____ c. Bjarni gave up seafaring because he was tired of it.

5. Understanding Main Ideas

One of the statements below expresses the main idea of the passage. One statement is too general, or too broad. The other explains only part of the passage; it is too narrow. Label the statements M for *main idea*, B for *too broad*, and N for *too narrow*.

_____ a. Bjarni Herjulfsson found new lands to the west of Greenland but did not explore them.

_____ b. Bjarni saw an unfamiliar land of low, wooded shores.

_____ c. The Vikings were famous for their seafaring skills.

Correct Answers, Part A _____

Correct Answers, Part B _____

Total Correct Answers _____

Elephants are the largest living land animals. Their size and the thickness and toughness of their skins protect them from most other wild animals. Since they have few enemies to fear, elephants are usually peaceful and easygoing. They become aggressive when their young are threatened. However, they show great affection for one another, and females spend their lives as members of a family herd. This is made up of several generations of relatives, with occasional additions by mating from other herds.

At birth, a baby elephant is about 3 feet (0.9 meter) tall and weighs about 200 pounds (91 kilograms). Its sparse coat of woolly hair gradually disappears. The young elephant is nursed by its mother for about two years and remains under her protection for two years more. Female elephants, as a rule, bear young once every four or five years.

The typical elephant herd contains from 20 to 40 females (cows) of all ages. Only males that are nursing remain with the cows. The leader is usually a mature cow. Adult males (bulls) usually live alone or in temporary all-male groups of up to seven members.

Elephants are active during both the day and the night, though they normally rest during the hottest hours of the day. During that time, the members of a family herd huddle together in any shade they can find and sleep standing up. Toward sundown, the herd walks to the nearest river, lake, or water hole to drink and bathe. The pace is set so that even the very young and the very old can keep up. If a mother with a baby falls behind, several other members of the herd will remain to protect them.

As the herd straggles along, the elephants push down young trees or uproot them with their tusks to feed on the tender roots, twigs, and leaves. In the open meadows, they gather up tufts of grass with their trunks and stuff them into their mouths. At times, a herd will invade the fields of farmers, but most will never enter villages or destroy huts.

A herd may range over a 50-mile (80-kilometer) radius in the course of a season. Seldom does the herd sleep in the same place for two days in succession. Pictures have been taken from airplanes showing vast elephant armies made up of many family herds traveling over the same route toward new feeding grounds.

Reading Time _____

Recalling Facts

1. Elephants are the
   - ❏ a. most aggressive land animals.
   - ❏ b. largest land animals.
   - ❏ c. tallest land animals.

2. Young elephants are protected by their mothers for
   - ❏ a. a week or so.
   - ❏ b. up to two years.
   - ❏ c. up to four years.

3. The typical elephant herd contains
   - ❏ a. adult males and females.
   - ❏ b. mostly males.
   - ❏ c. females and nursing young.

4. Elephants sleep
   - ❏ a. at night.
   - ❏ b. during the hottest hours of the day.
   - ❏ c. in the early morning.

5. Elephant herds tend to
   - ❏ a. live together in one place.
   - ❏ b. wander over a wide range.
   - ❏ c. break up into smaller groups.

Understanding Ideas

6. The members of an elephant herd can be described as
   - ❏ a. supportive.
   - ❏ b. selfish.
   - ❏ c. aggressive.

7. The organization of an elephant herd is based on
   - ❏ a. a pecking order.
   - ❏ b. family relationships.
   - ❏ c. a power structure.

8. It is likely that elephants eat
   - ❏ a. large amounts of food.
   - ❏ b. sparingly.
   - ❏ c. mostly animals and fish.

9. You can conclude from the article that elephants travel extensively in order to
   - ❏ a. get enough exercise.
   - ❏ b. protect their young.
   - ❏ c. find enough food.

10. Elephants can push down or uproot trees, which suggests that
    - ❏ a. they do not like trees.
    - ❏ b. they are very strong.
    - ❏ c. they are in a hurry to eat.

Death of an Elephant

The sick elephant cow stood apart from her herd. Her head was lowered, and her great ears flopped forward. A bull elephant approached her, sniffed her with his trunk, and returned to his feeding. For a while, the cow did not move. Then she dropped to her haunches without a sound. Immediately, the entire herd thundered toward her, screaming and trumpeting. As the sick cow slumped onto her stomach, the herd formed a circle around her.

The bull pushed larger elephants away from the dying cow, but he let young elephants touch her. One young bull laid his trunk across her back. The old bull lowered his head to her side and tried to lift her up. Then he tore up a trunkful of dried grass and pushed it into her mouth. She did not move.

The cow was almost gone now. With a great shudder, she fell onto her side. The herd began to trumpet again, as if their noise could bring her back to life. Then they moved off to feed restlessly nearby.

The old bull stayed beside the dead cow for a long while. From time to time, he tried to rouse her. One by one, other members of the herd returned to her body. Then, at dusk, the herd moved away together, leaving her alone.

1. **Recognizing Words in Context**

   Find the word *trumpet* in the passage. One definition below is a *synonym* for that word; it means the same or almost the same thing. One definition is an *antonym;* it has the opposite or nearly opposite meaning. The other has a completely different meaning. Label the definitions S for *synonym,* A for *antonym,* and D for *different.*

   _____ a. musical instrument

   _____ b. whisper

   _____ c. blare

2. **Distinguishing Fact from Opinion**

   Two of the statements below present *facts,* which can be proved correct. The other statement is an *opinion,* which expresses someone's thoughts or beliefs. Label the statements F for *fact* and O for *opinion.*

   _____ a. Elephants are caring animals.

   _____ b. The bull elephant tried to rouse the dying cow.

   _____ c. A young elephant laid his trunk across the cow's back.

3. Keeping Events in Order

Two of the statements below describe events that happened at the same time. The other statement describes an event that happened before or after those events. Label them S for *same time,* B for *before,* and A for *after.*

_____ a. The cow elephant dropped onto her stomach.

_____ b. The dying cow fell onto her haunches.

_____ c. The herd formed a circle around the dying cow.

4. Making Correct Inferences

Two of the statements below are correct *inferences,* or reasonable guesses. They are based on information in the passage. The other statement is an incorrect, or faulty, inference. Label the statements C for *correct* inference and F for *faulty* inference.

_____ a. The elephants were aware that something was wrong with the dying cow.

_____ b. The elephants knew how to make the sick cow better.

_____ c. The elephants were upset that the cow was dying.

5. Understanding Main Ideas

One of the statements below expresses the main idea of the passage. One statement is too general, or too broad. The other explains only part of the passage; it is too narrow. Label the statements M for *main idea,* B for *too broad,* and N for *too narrow.*

_____ a. Elephants are among the most intelligent mammals.

_____ b. A dying elephant's herd tried to help her.

_____ c. The old bull put food into the dying cow's mouth.

Correct Answers, Part A _____

Correct Answers, Part B _____

Total Correct Answers _____

Very early on, people must have felt the need to send messages and keep records. A cave dweller made little piles of stones to mark the boundaries of her land. A farmer made scratches on stones to mark the number of days since the full moon. Other scratches told a shepherd the number of skins a neighbor owed him. Villagers learned to communicate with distant places using a code of smoke signals or drumbeats. Hunters made pictures in sand and on the walls of caves.

From picture writing, called pictographs, the development of writing progressed in two ways. One, some of the pictures were simplified and given broader meanings. Thus, a person could write in pictures without having to draw realistically. The pictures became more abstract, a method similar to one that uses a stick figure to represent a human being. Two, a few designs were chosen from the pictographs and were used to represent the sounds of language, and these became an alphabet.

The development of pictures being turned into letters made it possible for more people to learn to write and to read. This development also enabled people to write quickly. It made it easier for one generation to pass on its best ideas to the next generation. An alphabet allowed people far apart to communicate easily and clearly. The recording of the great history of Western civilization was made possible by the early development of alphabetic writing.

In terms of writing, the marks on paper are not important in themselves. They are important for what they represent and for the job they do. That job is to make it possible for people to communicate with each other. To communicate with someone means that you can share your information, experiences, and emotions with that person. Something in one person's mind is put into written symbols so that another can share it. Perhaps it appears in the form of a poem, which is to be read and enjoyed by many people. Perhaps it is only a person's note to a friend, asking for help.

Writing speaks for the writer; it represents his or her thinking. It can never be any better than the writer. If the writer is not thinking in a clear and organized manner, he or she will not write effectively. If the writer does not know the subject, his or her writing will show this ignorance.

Reading Time _____

Recalling Facts

1. Early villagers communicated with distant places by using
   - ❏ a. a code of drumbeats.
   - ❏ b. sand pictures.
   - ❏ c. piles of stones.

2. Pictographs are
   - ❏ a. smoke signals.
   - ❏ b. picture writing.
   - ❏ c. letters.

3. The development of pictures into letters resulted in
   - ❏ a. the alphabet.
   - ❏ b. Western civilization.
   - ❏ c. reading.

4. The alphabet represents
   - ❏ a. coded signals.
   - ❏ b. communication.
   - ❏ c. the sounds of language.

5. Written symbols enable people to
   - ❏ a. share information.
   - ❏ b. speak more clearly.
   - ❏ c. be honest.

Understanding Ideas

6. The symbol $, which stands for money, is an example of
   - ❏ a. a realistic picture.
   - ❏ b. a pictograph.
   - ❏ c. a letter.

7. The article wants you to understand that without communication,
   - ❏ a. writing is pointless.
   - ❏ b. people cannot think.
   - ❏ c. people could not share ideas.

8. It is likely that early cave drawings were made to
   - ❏ a. keep records or tell a story.
   - ❏ b. send messages to distant places.
   - ❏ c. develop an alphabet.

9. The article suggests that the importance of writing is dependent on
   - ❏ a. whether it can be passed on to future generations.
   - ❏ b. how well it is written.
   - ❏ c. how well it communicates.

10. A successful computer manual was most likely written by
    - ❏ a. a person familiar with computers.
    - ❏ b. a person who is knowledgeable about art.
    - ❏ c. a person who is just learning about computers.

David Stuart's parents were archaeologists. They specialized in the Maya, who lived in Central America five hundred or more years ago. Every summer they took David with them to Central America while they worked there.

The meanings of Maya writing symbols had been lost. Scholars were trying to read the writing, but progress was slow. One day when David was twelve, his parents gave him a copy of some Maya writing to look at. The scholars had taken five years to figure it out. David deciphered it all in one day.

David worked with the Maya scholars all summer. Then he went back to junior high school, but he kept thinking about Maya writing. He figured out some important glyphs, as Maya writing symbols are called. At a meeting of Maya experts from all over the world, he presented his findings. He was only thirteen, but he had done something no one else had done.

By the time he graduated from high school, David Stuart was one of the leading experts in Maya writing. His brilliant work helped scholars read much new Maya writing. We now know that Maya writing contains rich and wonderful stories about Mayan kings and gods.

1. **Recognizing Words in Context**

   Find the word *deciphered* in the passage. One definition below is a *synonym* for that word; it means the same or almost the same thing. One definition is an *antonym;* it has the opposite or nearly opposite meaning. The other has a completely different meaning. Label the definitions S for *synonym*, A for *antonym*, and D for *different*.

   _____ a. encoded

   _____ b. figured out

   _____ c. discouraged

2. **Distinguishing Fact from Opinion**

   Two of the statements below present *facts,* which can be proved correct. The other statement is an *opinion*, which expresses someone's thoughts or beliefs. Label the statements F for *fact* and O for *opinion*.

   _____ a. The Maya lived in Central America five hundred years ago.

   _____ b. David Stuart's parents were archaeologists.

   _____ c. David's work on Maya writing was brilliant.

3. Keeping Events in Order

Label the statements below 1, 2, and 3 to show the order in which the events happened.

_____ a. David worked on Maya writing while he attended junior high school.

_____ b. David presented his findings at a meeting of Maya experts.

_____ c. David's parents gave him a copy of Maya writing.

4. Making Correct Inferences

Two of the statements below are correct *inferences*, or reasonable guesses. They are based on information in the passage. The other statement is an incorrect, or faulty, inference. Label the statements C for *correct* inference and F for *faulty* inference.

_____ a. Maya writing is difficult to read.

_____ b. David was a leading Maya expert at the age of thirteen.

_____ c. David Stuart had an exceptional talent for reading Mayan.

5. Understanding Main Ideas

One of the statements below expresses the main idea of the passage. One statement is too general, or too broad. The other explains only part of the passage; it is too narrow. Label the statements M for *main idea*, B for *too broad*, and N for *too narrow*.

_____ a. People are learning to read ancient writing symbols.

_____ b. David Stuart deciphered in one day what it had taken scholars five years to figure out.

_____ c. The work done by David Stuart as a teenager advanced the understanding of Maya writing.

Correct Answers, Part A _____

Correct Answers, Part B _____

Total Correct Answers _____

8　A　　D Is for Delta

In Greek, the English letter *D* is a delta. In print, a delta looks like a triangle. The ancient Greeks gave the letter's name to the similarly shaped areas of sediment set down at the mouths of rivers.

Rivers often carry large amounts of soil, sand, and other matter in their waters. When a river runs swiftly, its strong current erodes earth from the banks and carries it along with the current. As the river slows, some of this sediment settles. When a river flows into the sea, its current is abruptly slowed. The sediment tends to drop faster than when the river is flowing freely. Over the centuries, this sediment builds up into generally fan-shaped plains.

As the delta grows, the course of the river becomes blocked by buildup. The river then splits into a network of smaller branches before it empties into the sea.

Deltas form most often where a river carries a heavy load of suspended matter and where the sea is calm. Seas with strong tides and shore currents tend to wash away the sediment as fast as it is deposited. The Amazon River has a large underwater delta, but tides and waves keep the deposit from reaching sea level. Deltas are not present in regions such as the Atlantic coast of North America where the land has sunk or subsided in recent geologic times. The St. Lawrence and Hudson Rivers have bays called estuaries instead of deltas at their mouths.

Deltas have been of great benefit to humans since ancient times. The silts, sands, and clays left by floodwaters have proved very fertile. As humans learned to farm, great cities have sprung up in delta plains.

The mazes of waterways common in a delta provide natural routes for both communication and trade. River mouths give ocean vessels access to inner ports. Many of the world's great port cities are located in delta plains. Alexandria in Egypt and New Orleans in Louisiana are both flourishing examples.

The majority of the world's delta areas have not been used to their full economic potential. The Mekong Delta is known as the rice bowl of Southeast Asia because of the massive rice fields and farms there. However, political and military upheavals in the 1960s and 1970s delayed programs to increase the use of this fertile region. Other large tropical deltas in South America and Africa are, in essence, untouched.

Reading Time _____

Recalling Facts

1. A delta is
   - ❏ a. an area of sediment set down at the mouth of a river.
   - ❏ b. any fan-shaped body of water.
   - ❏ c. where the sea meets a landmass.

2. Deltas exist
   - ❏ a. at the mouths of most rivers.
   - ❏ b. where the ocean has strong currents.
   - ❏ c. where the sea is calm at the mouth of a river.

3. Deltas are not present
   - ❏ a. at the mouths of the St. Lawrence and Hudson Rivers.
   - ❏ b. in South America.
   - ❏ c. on the African coast.

4. The Mekong Delta is known as
   - ❏ a. Southeast Asia's biggest port.
   - ❏ b. the capital of Southeast Asia.
   - ❏ c. the rice bowl of Southeast Asia.

5. Alexandria, Egypt, and New Orleans, Louisiana, are examples of
   - ❏ a. great port cities not located in delta plains.
   - ❏ b. great port cities located in delta plains.
   - ❏ c. cities that are not great ports.

Understanding Ideas

6. You can conclude from the article that a slow-moving river
   - ❏ a. will most likely form a delta.
   - ❏ b. is not likely to form a delta.
   - ❏ c. has a large underwater delta.

7. It is likely that early settlers chose delta areas because
   - ❏ a. the fertile soil there encouraged farming.
   - ❏ b. great cities were built there.
   - ❏ c. delta soil was easy to plow.

8. Deltas are generally fan-shaped, which suggests that
   - ❏ a. buildup at the edges pushes sediments to the center.
   - ❏ b. buildup in the center pushes sediments to the edges.
   - ❏ c. sediments flow evenly as the river empties into the sea.

9. No deltas exist along the Atlantic coast of North America because
   - ❏ a. any sediment deposited cannot reach sea level.
   - ❏ b. of strong tides and currents.
   - ❏ c. the area is undeveloped.

10. It is likely that areas with undeveloped deltas
    - ❏ a. are better off leaving the deltas untouched.
    - ❏ b. could benefit economically if they were developed.
    - ❏ c. are too remote to be developed successfully.

Harvesting Rice

It was harvest time in the Mekong Delta. At the beginning of the rainy season, the rice seedlings had been planted by hand. Trang and other young women had lined up ankle deep in the water of the flooded paddy field. Taking one seedling at a time, Trang had worked, stooped over, gently pushing each plant into the mud. Now the rice had ripened. Its golden stalks were ready to be cut.

Singing joyous harvest songs, Trang and her friends paddled their small boats quickly down the narrow canal to the paddy fields. The teenagers shouted happily as their boats almost collided, almost swamped—but never did.

Offerings of flowers, candles, and incense were made to the gods and goddesses who protect the earth and plants. Then the long, tiring work of harvest began. With a small sickle, Trang cut the rice stalks. She bound the stalks into sheaves and stacked them on a nearby boat. Other workers carried the sheaves to the threshing floor.

At noon, work stopped for a feast. Trang eagerly dipped her chopsticks into her bowl of rice, vegetables, and curried chicken. Then it was back to work. This would be a good harvest, with much rice to feed the people for the coming year.

1. **Recognizing Words in Context**

    Find the word *bound* in the passage. One definition below is a *synonym* for that word; it means the same or almost the same thing. One definition is an *antonym;* it has the opposite or nearly opposite meaning. The other has a completely different meaning. Label the definitions S for *synonym,* A for *antonym,* and D for *different.*

    _____ a. tied

    _____ b. leap

    _____ c. released

2. **Distinguishing Fact from Opinion**

    Two of the statements below present *facts,* which can be proved correct. The other statement is an *opinion,* which expresses someone's thoughts or beliefs. Label the statements F for *fact* and O for *opinion.*

    _____ a. Growing rice is one of the hardest jobs for farmers.

    _____ b. Each rice seedling is planted by hand.

    _____ c. Workers cut the rice plants with small sickles.

3. Keeping Events in Order

Two of the statements below describe events that happened at the same time. The other statement describes an event that happened before or after those events. Label them S for *same time*, B for *before*, and A for *after*.

_____ a. Teenagers paddled their boats down the canal.

_____ b. Trang cut the rice stalks with a small sickle.

_____ c. Trang and her friends sang joyous harvest songs.

4. Making Correct Inferences

Two of the statements below are correct *inferences*, or reasonable guesses. They are based on information in the passage. The other statement is an incorrect, or faulty, inference. Label the statements C for *correct* inference and F for *faulty* inference.

_____ a. Harvesting rice is a lot of fun for the teenagers involved.

_____ b. Rice is an important food for people of the Mekong Delta.

_____ c. Growing rice involves hard, tiring work.

5. Understanding Main Ideas

One of the statements below expresses the main idea of the passage. One statement is too general, or too broad. The other explains only part of the passage; it is too narrow. Label the statements M for *main idea*, B for *too broad*, and N for *too narrow*.

_____ a. Offerings were made to the gods and goddesses before the rice was harvested.

_____ b. Planting and harvesting rice involves the work of many people.

_____ c. The Mekong Delta is known as the rice bowl of Southeast Asia.

Correct Answers, Part A _____

Correct Answers, Part B _____

Total Correct Answers _____

Few people realize how much hard work and planning are needed to maintain even the smallest zoo. At the head of a zoo is the director. Under the director are curators who have charge of different departments—a curator of birds, a curator of reptiles, and so on. Every large zoo has a hospital under the direction of a veterinarian. The animals are fed, and their living quarters are cleaned by keepers. Keepers are very important zoo workers. The well-being and good health of the animals depend largely upon how well the keepers care for them. Often there is a deep bond between these people and their wild charges.

Zoo directors go to endless trouble and great expense to provide for the animals and keep them in perfect health. Each animal is given the "climate" to which it is accustomed. Penguins live in a great refrigerated room with an icy swimming pool. The Komodo dragon basks in a steamy glass-walled room where temperatures reach those of hot, humid summer days. Filtered fresh air flows through the buildings because animals become irritable in stale, impure air. Since apes are very likely to catch colds and other human diseases, they are separated from the public as soon as symptoms of illness appear.

Every animal is provided a sleeping place that resembles as closely as possible the one that it would naturally choose. It might be a tree, a log, or some brush or leaves in which it may hide. This sleeping place gives the animal needed privacy and concealment. In the raccoon cage is a fountain of bubbling water, because these animals are accustomed to washing their food in a running stream. The elephant may scratch its wrinkled hide against a great rough-surfaced pillar. The fox is provided with brushwood on which it may brush its glossy coat, just as it does in the wild. The monkeys have bars, ropes, swings, and automobile tires to play on.

Animals may have their own pets. An elephant in the San Diego Zoo was devoted to a black Shetland pony that shared its living quarters. Monkeys and apes become very fond of their keepers, but so do many other animals. The San Diego Zoo had a sick baby walrus that after each feeding fell asleep with its head on its keeper's lap. The keeper always stayed until he could slip away without disturbing the walrus.

Reading Time _____

Recalling Facts

1. Zoos are maintained by
   - ❏ a. state governments.
   - ❏ b. organizations of workers.
   - ❏ c. volunteers.

2. Injured and diseased animals are treated by
   - ❏ a. veterinarians.
   - ❏ b. curators.
   - ❏ c. keepers.

3. Workers responsible for the daily care of animals are
   - ❏ a. directors.
   - ❏ b. veterinarians.
   - ❏ c. keepers.

4. An animal's sleeping place should provide
   - ❏ a. privacy.
   - ❏ b. running water.
   - ❏ c. playthings.

5. Animals become irritable when
   - ❏ a. their sleep is disturbed.
   - ❏ b. they are fed.
   - ❏ c. they breathe stale, impure air.

Understanding Ideas

6. Animals in zoos are healthier when
   - ❏ a. their environment is similar to their environment in the wild.
   - ❏ b. they are separated from each other.
   - ❏ c. they have their own pets.

7. An important factor in an animal's environment is
   - ❏ a. space.
   - ❏ b. temperature.
   - ❏ c. lighting.

8. You can conclude from the article that the Komodo dragon's natural environment is
   - ❏ a. very cold and damp.
   - ❏ b. hot and humid.
   - ❏ c. desertlike.

9. You can conclude from the article that humans and animals
   - ❏ a. share common needs.
   - ❏ b. are natural enemies.
   - ❏ c. have nothing in common.

10. The article suggests that zoo workers are
    - ❏ a. bored with their jobs.
    - ❏ b. well paid.
    - ❏ c. caring people.

Can a gorilla love a kitten? One 230-pound (104-kilogram) lowland gorilla named Koko did. Koko was part of a study in which gorillas were taught American Sign Language, the system of communication used by many hearing-impaired people. Koko learned and used more than 500 signs and understood another 500 signs.

Koko was fascinated by cats. "The Three Little Kittens" and "Puss in Boots" were two of her favorite stories. One day, Koko signed to her trainer, Dr. Francine Patterson, that she wanted a cat. Dr. Patterson gave Koko a toy cat, but she just pouted. It was obvious that this was not what Koko had meant. When someone brought three abandoned kittens to the center where Koko lived, Koko signed, "Love that," so Dr. Patterson let her pick one for a pet. Koko's choice was a male kitten with no tail. She named him All Ball.

Koko treated her kitten as she would have treated a baby gorilla. She carried him tucked against herself or held him gently and petted him. As a child would, she even dressed her pet in napkins and hats! The huge gorilla and the tiny kitten enjoyed playing chase together, as well as Koko's favorite game, tickling.

As Koko held her pet, she often signed, "Soft good cat cat."

1. **Recognizing Words in Context**

   Find the word *fascinated* in the passage. One definition below is a *synonym* for that word; it means the same or almost the same thing. One definition is an *antonym;* it has the opposite or nearly opposite meaning. The other has a completely different meaning. Label the definitions S for *synonym,* A for *antonym,* and D for *different.*

   _____ a. attracted

   _____ b. spellbound

   _____ c. repelled

2. **Distinguishing Fact from Opinion**

   Two of the statements below present *facts,* which can be proved correct. The other statement is an *opinion,* which expresses someone's thoughts or beliefs. Label the statements F for *fact* and O for *opinion.*

   _____ a. Koko communicated by using American Sign Language.

   _____ b. Zoos and other places where gorillas are kept in captivity should give them pets.

   _____ c. Koko treated her kitten gently.

3. Keeping Events in Order

Two of the statements below describe events that happened at the same time. The other statement describes an event that happened before or after those events. Label them S for *same time,* B for *before,* and A for *after.*

_____ a. Koko named her tailless kitten All Ball.

_____ b. Koko held her kitten.

_____ c. Koko often signed, "Soft good cat cat."

4. Making Correct Inferences

Two of the statements below are correct *inferences,* or reasonable guesses. They are based on information in the passage. The other statement is an incorrect, or faulty, inference. Label the statements C for *correct* inference and F for *faulty* inference.

_____ a. A gorilla can treat another animal with gentleness and love.

_____ b. All gorillas would enjoy having kittens for pets.

_____ c. Gorillas can be taught to communicate with humans by using sign language.

5. Understanding Main Ideas

One of the statements below expresses the main idea of the passage. One statement is too general, or too broad. The other explains only part of the passage; it is too narrow. Label the statements M for *main idea,* B for *too broad,* and N for *too narrow.*

_____ a. As part of an ongoing study of language in apes, gorillas were taught American Sign Language.

_____ b. Koko was fascinated by cats.

_____ c. Koko, a 230-pound (104-kilogram) lowland gorilla, had a pet kitten.

Correct Answers, Part A _____

Correct Answers, Part B _____

Total Correct Answers _____

An important thing to consider when buying a dog is whether it will fit comfortably into your living quarters when it reaches adult size. The presence of young children in the family should also be a factor in selection. A dog for a growing family must be able to stand rough treatment. A toy dog would be a poor choice for such a family because its tiny bones are fragile enough to break when children handle it roughly. In general, larger dogs, such as Labrador retrievers or German shepherds, are better adapted both physically and temperamentally for a young family.

A dog can be acquired from many sources. It can be bought from a reputable pet shop or from a kennel. Newspaper advertisements describe pups for sale from private parties. Local humane societies have dogs available, too. From whatever source you get a dog, however, make certain it is healthy. Ask for proof, if possible, that it has received all the necessary immunizing shots.

Males are usually larger, stronger, and more aggressive, and they make excellent watchdogs. On the other hand, females are usually more affectionate and gentle, and if they are purebred dogs and are mated with males of their breed, their pups can be sold for profit. The female has a strong maternal instinct and will guard children as well as she does her own pups.

Should you buy a purebred or a mongrel? This question is hard to answer because a purebred dog sometimes turns out to be less desirable than expected, while a mongrel often makes an alert, intelligent, and delightful family pet. As a rule, a purebred pup inherits the traits of its breed. As a result, few surprises in body form and temperament arise when the pup reaches adulthood. If you want to buy a purebred but are unfamiliar with the breed, first look at a full-grown dog of the breed. The puppy will grow to resemble it. If you want to buy a mongrel, try to see its sire and dam. Its parents will display any unwanted trait that may lie hidden in the puppy.

Ideally, children and puppies should grow up together. Caution should be taken, however, when dog owners bring a newborn baby home. Pampered dogs sometimes resent the newcomer because the baby receives most of the parents' attention. They should make an effort to pay attention to the dog, too.

Reading Time _____

Recalling Facts

1. Toy dogs are inappropriate for young families because they
   - ❏ a. are always hungry.
   - ❏ b. cost more.
   - ❏ c. cannot stand rough treatment.

2. Dogs bought as pets should have
   - ❏ a. been purchased from a kennel.
   - ❏ b. received all their immunizing shots.
   - ❏ c. a loud bark.

3. Female dogs tend to be
   - ❏ a. excellent watchdogs.
   - ❏ b. affectionate guardians.
   - ❏ c. restless.

4. The temperament of a purebred pup is
   - ❏ a. likely to resemble that of its breed.
   - ❏ b. unpredictable.
   - ❏ c. preferable to that of a mongrel.

5. When buying a mongrel, would-be owners should
   - ❏ a. study pictures of its sire and dam.
   - ❏ b. consider its coloration.
   - ❏ c. see its sire and dam.

Understanding Ideas

6. You can conclude from the article that dogs
   - ❏ a. can feel jealousy.
   - ❏ b. have no feelings.
   - ❏ c. respond negatively to new situations.

7. The article suggests that mongrel dogs
   - ❏ a. do not make good pets.
   - ❏ b. may be more desirable than purebreds.
   - ❏ c. can never be as desirable as purebreds.

8. The article wants you understand that deciding what dog to own
   - ❏ a. is best left to chance.
   - ❏ b. requires careful consideration.
   - ❏ c. depends mainly on what is affordable.

9. A very large dog would probably be most suitable for
   - ❏ a. a large family.
   - ❏ b. a single person living in an apartment.
   - ❏ c. an owner living in the country.

10. The article suggests that dogs
    - ❏ a. enjoy human companionship.
    - ❏ b. can adapt to almost any situation.
    - ❏ c. like living on their own.

10 B   The Bullfighting Dog

Mark Simmons walked toward the pasture where his twelve cows and a bull
were grazing. Trotting at his heels was his terrier, Sassy. Mark opened the
pasture gate and went in to open a second gate leading to a pen where he
had placed the animals' food. As Mark turned his back on the herd and
started to open the gate, the bull rammed him from the side! Mark was
slammed to the ground. His breath knocked out of him, Mark could barely
move. He knew his ribs were broken. Helplessly, he watched as the bull
lowered his massive head. Mark knew the bull was going to gore him with
his horns.

Coming out of nowhere, Sassy flew at the angry bull! She clamped her
teeth onto the bull's nose and hung there for a few seconds. She held on
long enough to distract the bull from the injured farmer. Then she dropped
to the ground. The bull shook his head and walked away.

Sassy leaned over her owner and licked his face. Painfully, Mark got up.
Holding his injured ribcage, he managed to make it to the house. "Call
911," he told his wife. Then he patted Sassy and said, "You just saved my
life, girl."

1. **Recognizing Words in Context**

Find the word *barely* in the passage.
One definition below is a *synonym* for
that word; it means the same or
almost the same thing. One definition
is an *antonym;* it has the opposite or
nearly opposite meaning. The other
has a completely different meaning.
Label the definitions S for *synonym,* A
for *antonym,* and D for *different.*

_____ a. totally

_____ b. nakedly

_____ c. scarcely

2. **Distinguishing Fact from Opinion**

Two of the statements below present
facts, which can be proved correct.
The other statement is an *opinion,*
which expresses someone's thoughts
or beliefs. Label the statements F for
fact and O for *opinion.*

_____ a. Sassy bit the bull in the
nose.

_____ b. The bull rammed Mark and
slammed him to the
ground.

_____ c. You should never turn your
back on a bull.

3. Keeping Events in Order

Two of the statements below describe events that happened at the same time. The other statement describes an event that happened before or after those events. Label them S for *same time,* B for *before,* and A for *after.*

_____ a. Mark looked up helplessly at the bull.

_____ b. The bull lowered its head.

_____ c. Sassy licked Mark's face.

4. Making Correct Inferences

Two of the statements below are correct *inferences,* or reasonable guesses. They are based on information in the passage. The other statement is an incorrect, or faulty, inference. Label the statements C for *correct* inference and F for *faulty* inference.

_____ a. The bull was afraid of the dog.

_____ b. When he was attacked by Sassy, the bull forgot about attacking the farmer.

_____ c. Sassy knew that Mark was in danger from the bull.

5. Understanding Main Ideas

One of the statements below expresses the main idea of the passage. One statement is too general, or too broad. The other explains only part of the passage; it is too narrow. Label the statements M for *main idea,* B for *too broad,* and N for *too narrow.*

_____ a. Many brave dogs have risked their lives to save people in danger.

_____ b. Sassy clamped her teeth onto the bull's nose and hung there.

_____ c. A terrier named Sassy saved her owner, who was being attacked by a bull.

Correct Answers, Part A _____

Correct Answers, Part B _____

Total Correct Answers _____

Although they are closely related to cockroaches, termites are sometimes called ants because their general appearance and social organization are like those of the ants. Termites, however, are distinguished from ants by their soft bodies and lighter color. Ants have hard bodies and are usually dark.

More than 40 species of termites live in the United States. A typical colony lives underground in a damp, chamberlike nest. The colony is organized into a caste system with four different adult forms: royalty, nobility, soldiers, and workers. The royalty consists of the kings and queens, which carry on the work of reproduction. They have well-developed wings and eyes. The kings are usually smaller than the queens, which may reach a length of 4.3 inches (11 centimeters) in some species.

Once a year, pairs of young kings and queens depart from the parent nest, leaving the ruling king and queen behind. Each pair starts a new colony nearby. Within a short time, the young queens may begin laying eggs at the rate of 3,000 to 5,000 a day. The nobility consists of wingless or short-winged adults. They take over the work of reproduction if a king or queen should die.

The soldiers, who have large heads and jaws, guard the nest against insect enemies, chiefly ants. The workers keep the colony supplied with food, and they actually feed the queens, soldiers, and young termites.

Termites feed primarily on wood fiber, or cellulose, which they get from dead trees, rotting plant material in the soil, fence posts, house timbers, or furniture. Although some kinds of termites can and do destroy human dwellings, they serve a vital function in the food web by recycling the nutrients found in dead wood. The nutrients can then be used by bacteria and plants.

Once inside the woodwork of a building, termites tunnel in all directions, with no openings showing on the surface. Houses may be inspected for signs of termite problems by searching for hollow timbers, for termite nests at the base of wood, or for the insects themselves. Unfortunately, the first sign of their presence may be the collapse of a wall or some other wooden structure.

To rid an area of termites would require the destruction of all the nests. It is more practical to protect a building against the insects by treating woodwork with chemicals or by covering all possible points of attack with metal.

Reading Time _____

Recalling Facts

1. Termites are like ants in terms of
   - ❏ a. coloration.
   - ❏ b. general appearance and social organization.
   - ❏ c. the number of species.

2. The main enemy of termites is
   - ❏ a. birds.
   - ❏ b. worms.
   - ❏ c. ants.

3. If a king or queen should die, the work of reproduction is carried on by
   - ❏ a. workers.
   - ❏ b. royalty.
   - ❏ c. nobility.

4. Termites feed primarily on
   - ❏ a. sand.
   - ❏ b. cellulose.
   - ❏ c. plants.

5. A building can be protected against termites by
   - ❏ a. treating woodwork with chemicals.
   - ❏ b. recycling dead wood.
   - ❏ c. flooding nests with water.

Understanding Ideas

6. You can conclude from the article that the social organization of termites is
   - ❏ a. informal.
   - ❏ b. disorganized.
   - ❏ c. highly developed.

7. The social organization of a termite colony could best be compared to
   - ❏ a. the class system in Great Britain, which has a monarch and nobles.
   - ❏ b. the democratic system in the United States.
   - ❏ c. a master-slave system.

8. It is likely that queens lay so many eggs because
   - ❏ a. many young will not survive.
   - ❏ b. they know they will die in a short time.
   - ❏ c. most will be eaten by the kings.

9. You can conclude from the article that termites in a colony have different characteristics
   - ❏ a. according to their age.
   - ❏ b. to suit their function in the nest.
   - ❏ c. because of the food they eat.

10. Woodwork can be protected from termites by metal, which suggests that
   - ❏ a. metal is cheaper than woodwork.
   - ❏ b. chemicals will not always work.
   - ❏ c. termites cannot eat metal.

In Zimbabwe, South Africa, a company offered a prize to the architect who could design an office building for them. The catch was that the building had to stay cool in summer and warm in winter, without air conditioning and with minimal heat, in a country whose temperature varies from 35 to 104 degrees Fahrenheit (2 to 40 degrees Celsius). Architects from all over Africa competed. The winner copied the design of a termite mound.

South African termites eat only a certain fungus that grows at exactly 67 degrees Fahrenheit (20 degrees Celsius). They build huge mounds of earth with cool mud inside and air vents all around. Air blowing across the mud provides a natural air conditioning. The termites constantly plug and unplug the vents to keep the temperature even inside the mounds.

The winning architect designed a building similar to the termite mound. It has few windows, and it's shaded so the sun cannot heat it. It is built around a shady, cool, central area. Fans suck out the heat and blow cool air through the hollow floors.

The office building is a success. It was cheaper to build than similar buildings, and it is cheaper to maintain. Its cooling system works well, just like that of the South African termite mounds.

1. **Recognizing Words in Context**

   Find the word *minimal* in the passage. One definition below is a *synonym* for that word; it means the same or almost the same thing. One definition is an *antonym*; it has the opposite or nearly opposite meaning. The other has a completely different meaning. Label the definitions S for *synonym*, A for *antonym*, and D for *different*.

   _____ a. much

   _____ b. little

   _____ c. natural

2. **Distinguishing Fact from Opinion**

   Two of the statements below present *facts*, which can be proved correct. The other statement is an *opinion*, which expresses someone's thoughts or beliefs. Label the statements F for *fact* and O for *opinion*.

   _____ a. Zimbabwe's air temperature varies from 35 to 104 degrees Fahrenheit (2 to 40 degrees Celsius).

   _____ b. The winning architect copied the design of a termite mound.

   _____ c. The office building is a success.

3. Keeping Events in Order

Label the statements below 1, 2, and 3 to show the order in which the events happened.

_____ a. The winning architect copied the cooling system of termite mounds.

_____ b. The building is cooled by fans.

_____ c. A company challenged architects to design an office building that would be comfortable without air conditioning.

4. Making Correct Inferences

Two of the statements below are correct *inferences,* or reasonable guesses. They are based on information in the passage. The other statement is an incorrect, or faulty, inference. Label the statements C for *correct* inference and F for *faulty* inference.

_____ a. Studying nature can lead to creative solutions to problems.

_____ b. Termite-mound air conditioning works better than mechanical air conditioning.

_____ c. The design of a termite mound can be adapted for use in modern building techniques.

5. Understanding Main Ideas

One of the statements below expresses the main idea of the passage. One statement is too general, or too broad. The other explains only part of the passage; it is too narrow. Label the statements M for *main idea,* B for *too broad,* and N for *too narrow.*

_____ a. Different kinds of air conditioning can cool structures.

_____ b. South African termites cool their earth mounds by opening and closing vents dug into the mounds.

_____ c. An architect used the cooling principles of a termite mound to cool an office building.

Correct Answers, Part A _____

Correct Answers, Part B _____

Total Correct Answers _____

Ending the Slave Trade

For 30 years, the American Anti-Slavery Movement was a powerful but divisive influence in the United States. It never had the support of a majority of Northerners. Most did not like its extremism. They knew that the Constitution left it to the states to decide about slavery. But they did not want to see the Union divided. The Northern states had abolished slavery between 1777 and 1804. However, many people in the North would not welcome a large black population. They feared that slaves would want to move to the North if freedom were available there and not in the South.

One thing the North would not permit was the extension of slavery into new states and territories. It was this issue that eventually led to the election of Abraham Lincoln as president. Next came the secession of the South from the Union and the Civil War. After the war, slavery was abolished by the Thirteenth Amendment to the Constitution.

Although slavery did not exist in the nations of western Europe, it did exist in their colonies. The French were the first to outlaw slavery in all their territories. In 1794, the French government freed all French slaves. Bloody uprisings in Haiti a few years later led Napoleon I, the emperor of France, to reestablish slavery there in 1802. By 1819, the French slave trade was outlawed. In 1848, slavery was banned for good in all French colonies.

In Latin America, slavery was abolished gradually, on a country-by-country basis. In Chile, the first antislavery law was passed as early as 1811. The slave trade was abolished and children born of slaves were freed. However, adult slaves were not freed until 1823. In Venezuela, abolition was also gradual, mostly because the government did not want to pay slave-holders all at once for the loss of their human property. Freed slaves were forced, as compensation, to work for former owners for a number of years. Slavery finally ended in South America in 1888 when Brazil passed an anti-slavery law.

The complete removal of slavery could not occur until all trading in slaves was abolished. With this in mind, the British and Foreign Anti-Slavery Society was founded in England in 1839. By 1862, international treaties allowing the right to search ocean vessels had been signed by most Western nations, including the United States. Within a few years, the slave trade was destroyed.

Reading Time _____

Recalling Facts

1. In the original Constitution, the decision about slavery was left to
   - ❏ a. the federal government.
   - ❏ b. the states.
   - ❏ c. slave owners.

2. The issue that led to Lincoln's election as president was
   - ❏ a. the extension of slavery into new states and territories.
   - ❏ b. the secession of the South.
   - ❏ c. international treaties.

3. The first western European nation to outlaw slavery in all its territories was
   - ❏ a. England.
   - ❏ b. France.
   - ❏ c. Spain.

4. Slavery ended in South America when an antislavery law was passed in
   - ❏ a. Venezuela.
   - ❏ b. Chile.
   - ❏ c. Brazil.

5. The slave trade was finally destroyed in the
   - ❏ a. seventeenth century.
   - ❏ b. eighteenth century.
   - ❏ c. nineteenth century.

Understanding Ideas

6. In electing Lincoln president, Americans cast their votes for
   - ❏ a. slavery.
   - ❏ b. the Constitution.
   - ❏ c. the abolishment of slavery.

7. The North's attitude toward freed slaves could be described as
   - ❏ a. heartfelt.
   - ❏ b. hypocritical.
   - ❏ c. benevolent.

8. You can conclude from the article that slave owners considered slaves as
   - ❏ a. family members.
   - ❏ b. property.
   - ❏ c. people with rights.

9. The slave issue in the United States was ultimately decided by the
   - ❏ a. South's secession from the Union.
   - ❏ b. death of Abraham Lincoln.
   - ❏ c. outcome of the Civil War.

10. The slow removal of slavery around the world suggests that
    - ❏ a. people are resistant to change.
    - ❏ b. those who were against slavery were slow to act.
    - ❏ c. slaves did not want to be freed.

Of the thirteen original states that ratified the United States Constitution in 1789, all but three had already banned the importation of slaves from other countries. From the beginning, there was great resistance to slavery in Congress, but there were too few votes to outlaw it directly. In 1794, Congress did pass a law forbidding the outfitting of slave ships in the United States, as well as the exporting of slaves. And by 1798 no state was importing slaves from other countries.

In 1793, however, Eli Whitney had invented the cotton gin for removing seeds from raw cotton. It became very profitable to grow large quantities of cotton. South Carolina, in need of workers, reopened its harbors to foreign slavers in 1803. South Carolina's delegates argued that their state's economy could not survive without slaves.

South Carolina won the debate, but reaction from other states was harsh and negative. Legislation to end the slave trade was introduced in 1804, 1805, and 1806. Each time, it failed—but by narrower and narrower margins. In 1807, a bill to end the slave trade passed the House by a vote of 113 to 5. President Jefferson signed it into law, and in 1808 it went into effect. Historians now feel that this was the first step toward abolishing slavery in America.

1. **Recognizing Words in Context**

   Find the word *ratified* in the passage. One definition below is a *synonym* for that word; it means the same or almost the same thing. One definition is an *antonym;* it has the opposite or nearly opposite meaning. The other has a completely different meaning. Label the definitions S for *synonym,* A for *antonym,* and D for *different.*

   _____ a. rejected

   _____ b. wrote

   _____ c. endorsed

2. **Distinguishing Fact from Opinion**

   Two of the statements below present *facts,* which can be proved correct. The other statement is an *opinion,* which expresses someone's thoughts or beliefs. Label the statements F for *fact* and O for *opinion.*

   _____ a. From the beginning, there was great resistance to slavery.

   _____ b. A bill to end the slave trade passed in 1807.

   _____ c. By 1798, no state was importing slaves.

3. Keeping Events in Order

Label the statements below 1, 2, and 3 to show the order in which the events happened.

_____ a. South Carolina reopened its harbors to foreign slave ships.

_____ b. President Jefferson signed a bill outlawing the importing of slaves.

_____ c. Congress passed a law forbidding the exporting of slaves from the United States.

4. Making Correct Inferences

Two of the statements below are correct *inferences,* or reasonable guesses. They are based on information in the passage. The other statement is an incorrect, or faulty, inference. Label the statements C for *correct* inference and F for *faulty* inference.

_____ a. Most of the original states were against the practice of slavery.

_____ b. Congress was persistent in trying to end the slave trade.

_____ c. Early Congresses did not attempt to fight slavery.

5. Understanding Main Ideas

One of the statements below expresses the main idea of the passage. One statement is too general, or too broad. The other explains only part of the passage; it is too narrow. Label the statements M for *main idea,* B for *too broad,* and N for *too narrow.*

_____ a. The first step toward ending slavery in America was the political fight to end the slave trade.

_____ b. Congress tried to end the slave trade.

_____ c. Legislation introduced to end the slave trade in the early 1800s failed by narrower and narrower margins.

Correct Answers, Part A _____

Correct Answers, Part B _____

Total Correct Answers _____

The Roman writer Seneca once said, "All things are cause either for laughter or weeping." He understood that laughing and crying are closely related emotional responses to some kind of outside stimulation. He knew that in life, as in drama, comedy and tragedy are never far apart. Both laughing and crying serve to ease tension.

Laughter, like weeping, is a reflex action. It is rooted in the central nervous system and its related hormones. It is expressed in the contraction of certain facial muscles and in altered breathing patterns. The stimulation that brings forth laughter is called humor. Defining laughter and humor in this way, however, leaves two unanswered questions. Why do people laugh? What is funny, or humorous? The questions are difficult to answer because emotions and the reasons for them are not easily analyzed.

Something humorous does not amuse everyone. Sometimes the reason is cultural. Each society has its own notion of what is comic. An American viewing a British comedy may find little to laugh at because the origin of the humor is not understood. Even within one culture, there are different responses to humor. Young children, teenagers, and adults do not laugh at the same things.

Values and morals also affect people's views of humor. Prior to the civil rights movement, ethnic humor was popular in the United States. But the resurgence of ethnic pride in the early 1960s virtually ended the widespread use of such humor. Telling ethnic stories through the public media became risky unless the teller was a member of the group about which the stories were told.

Humor appeals primarily to two senses—hearing and seeing. Before television, professional comics on radio had to rely on words and sounds alone to convey humor. When an audience can see a performer on stage, in movies, or on television, both verbal humor and visual humor are possible.

Humor in the form of words may be either written or spoken. One of the most common kinds of verbal humor is the play on words. This type includes puns, riddles, and some limericks. Of all types of verbal humor, the joke, or witticism, is probably the most popular.

Almost anything that can be seen may be perceived as humorous by someone, even if it was intended to be serious. Visual humor often relies on transforming the normal or serious into the unexpected, ridiculous, or absurd.

Reading Time _____

Recalling Facts

1. Laughter is expressed by changes in
   - ❏ a. facial muscles and breathing patterns.
   - ❏ b. eye movement and facial muscles.
   - ❏ c. breathing patterns and body temperature.

2. The stimulation that leads to laughter is called
   - ❏ a. giggling.
   - ❏ b. humor.
   - ❏ c. joking.

3. What is considered humorous depends greatly on
   - ❏ a. cultural background.
   - ❏ b. the influence of television.
   - ❏ c. internal tension.

4. Humor appeals primarily to the senses of
   - ❏ a. hearing and smell.
   - ❏ b. hearing and seeing.
   - ❏ c. seeing and touch.

5. The most popular type of verbal humor is probably the
   - ❏ a. ethnic joke.
   - ❏ b. limerick.
   - ❏ c. witticism.

Understanding Ideas

6. Laughing and crying can be considered
   - ❏ a. the same emotion.
   - ❏ b. involuntary emotions.
   - ❏ c. unrelated emotional responses.

7. Laughing and crying are caused by
   - ❏ a. humorous tension.
   - ❏ b. the same stimulation.
   - ❏ c. different stimulations.

8. Unlike radio comics, comics who perform on television have to consider
   - ❏ a. the visual dimensions of humor.
   - ❏ b. the power of verbal humor.
   - ❏ c. how sounds convey humor.

9. What is considered humorous depends mainly on
   - ❏ a. how the humor is conveyed.
   - ❏ b. the perceptions of the audience.
   - ❏ c. timing.

10. Jokes that rely on the embarrassment of a particular group are
    - ❏ a. gaining in popularity.
    - ❏ b. no longer considered appropriate humor.
    - ❏ c. common in the media.

One of America's best-loved humorists was Will Rogers, a part-Cherokee cowboy noted for his folksy ways. Rogers was born in 1879 in Oologah, Indian Territory—now Oklahoma. He was an expert rider and roper. Billed as "The Cherokee Kid," Rogers twirled his lariat and made jokes in Wild West shows, vaudeville, and the Ziegfield Follies.

From his humble beginnings, Rogers went on to become a national star. Millions of people listened to his radio broadcasts, flocked to see his movies, and read his books and newspaper columns. During the 1920s, Rogers toured the country, speaking up for the common people and poking fun at bureaucracy. He was known for his good-natured but sharp political satire. Speaking in his slow western drawl and scratching his head, Rogers would let fall one-liners such as these: "It takes a great country to stand a thing like an election hitting it every four years." "I do not belong to an organized political party; I'm a Democrat."

In 1935, Rogers and his friend, aviator Wiley Post, were killed in a plane crash in Alaska. The entire country mourned the loss of the good-natured cowboy who had once said, "I never met a man I did not like."

1. **Recognizing Words in Context**

   Find the word *humble* in the passage. One definition below is a *synonym* for that word; it means the same or almost the same thing. One definition is an *antonym;* it has the opposite or nearly opposite meaning. The other has a completely different meaning. Label the definitions S for *synonym*, A for *antonym*, and D for *different*.

   _____ a. demean

   _____ b. unpretentious

   _____ c. luxurious

2. **Distinguishing Fact from Opinion**

   Two of the statements below present *facts*, which can be proved correct. The other statement is an *opinion*, which expresses someone's thoughts or beliefs. Label the statements F for *fact* and O for *opinion*.

   _____ a. Will Rogers was a part-Cherokee cowboy from Oklahoma.

   _____ b. Will Rogers became a well-known humorist and movie star.

   _____ c. Of all American humorists, Will Rogers was the most loved.

3. Keeping Events in Order

Label the statements below 1, 2, and 3 to show the order in which the events happened.

_____ a. Will Rogers was killed in a plane crash in Alaska.

_____ b. Rogers toured the country during the 1920s.

_____ c. Will Rogers was billed as "The Cherokee Kid" in Wild West shows.

4. Making Correct Inferences

Two of the statements below are correct *inferences,* or reasonable guesses. They are based on information in the passage. The other statement is an incorrect, or faulty, inference. Label the statements C for *correct* inference and F for *faulty* inference.

_____ a. Will Rogers was just a simple cowboy with a sense of humor.

_____ b. Beneath his humble ways, Will Rogers was a clever, witty man.

_____ c. People were drawn to Will Rogers because of his good nature.

5. Understanding Main Ideas

One of the statements below expresses the main idea of the passage. One statement is too general, or too broad. The other explains only part of the passage; it is too narrow. Label the statements M for *main idea,* B for *too broad,* and N for *too narrow.*

_____ a. Will Rogers told jokes in Wild West shows and vaudeville.

_____ b. Wild West shows were a popular form of entertainment in the 1800s and early 1900s.

_____ c. Will Rogers, a part-Cherokee cowboy, was one of America's best-loved humorists.

Correct Answers, Part A _____

Correct Answers, Part B _____

Total Correct Answers _____

Enjoy My Hospitality

The sending of invitations has long played an important role in the etiquette of hospitality. Among the first people to use invitations were the North American Indians. One of their methods was to burn messages in buckskin. These were then carried by runners to all the guests. In England in Shakespeare's time, invitations were written on large sheets of white paper and colorfully decorated. Pages or messengers carried them to the guests, who were usually required to answer. It was considered insulting to give invitations any other way. But today mailing and telephoning invitations are acceptable ways of getting guests together.

To early people, hospitality meant sharing food and shelter with friends or strangers. This has remained one of the chief ways of expressing friendship. Among the Bedouin Arabs, for example, it is considered ill mannered and insulting to ride up to a person's tent without stopping to eat with him or her. A ceremony of hospitality among the Bedouin is the coffee-brewing ritual. The host always makes a fresh pot, using elaborate utensils that are handed down from generation to generation. Another such ritual is the tea ceremony of Japan.

A guest in Japan is given small candies and cakes, which are served on pieces of paper. To be polite, the guest must wrap any leftover food in the paper and carry it away with him or her. In the United States, too, hosts often give their guests food to take home, such as a piece of cake from a birthday party.

Many other rituals have been used to make guests feel welcome. Early Greeks gave salt to a guest as a symbol of hospitality. In Arab lands today, guests must be careful not to admire a host's possessions. If they do, the host will offer the possessions to them. Among the North American Indians, smoking a tobacco pipe, the calumet, was the chief ritual of hospitality. Passing around the calumet became a feature of tribal gatherings for making peace or forging alliances.

Table manners evolved along with the development of hospitality. The ancient Greeks did not use knives, forks, or spoons for eating. They used their fingers to eat solid foods, which were cut into small pieces before being served. They drank liquids directly from cups or sopped them up with bread. The Romans did not use individual plates but took food with their fingers directly from the platters.

Reading Time _____

Recalling Facts

1. In Shakespeare's time, invitations were
   - ❏ a. sent by mail.
   - ❏ b. carried by messenger.
   - ❏ c. issued by telephone.

2. Coffee brewing is a ritual among
   - ❏ a. the Japanese.
   - ❏ b. Bedouin Arabs.
   - ❏ c. North American Indians.

3. A symbol of hospitality for early Greeks was
   - ❏ a. giving salt to a guest.
   - ❏ b. smoking a tobacco pipe.
   - ❏ c. bowing to a guest.

4. Eating utensils were
   - ❏ a. popular in early Rome.
   - ❏ b. used only by guests in early Greece and Rome.
   - ❏ c. unknown to early Greeks and Romans.

5. North American Indians smoked a peace pipe called a
   - ❏ a. calumet.
   - ❏ b. quarter.
   - ❏ c. condiment.

Understanding Ideas

6. You can conclude from the article that etiquette today is
   - ❏ a. more formal than in past times.
   - ❏ b. less formal than in past times.
   - ❏ c. nonexistent.

7. The concept of hospitality is
   - ❏ a. a new idea.
   - ❏ b. centuries old.
   - ❏ c. no longer considered important.

8. You can conclude from the article that hospitality is
   - ❏ a. mostly an issue of table manners.
   - ❏ b. delivering messages.
   - ❏ c. any way of making guests feel welcome.

9. The ritual of hospitality
   - ❏ a. is the same the world over.
   - ❏ b. varies from country to country.
   - ❏ c. always involves food.

10. Today the table manners of the ancient Greeks would be considered
    - ❏ a. refined.
    - ❏ b. courteous.
    - ❏ c. impolite.

The wife of Chief Yakotlus had given birth to a son. Among the Kwakiutl people of the Pacific Northwest, this was cause for a great celebration. In honor of his son's birth, the chief invited guests from near and far to a potlatch. Not only would he show off his heir, but he would also have a chance to display his wealth. Everyone who came would know what a great chief Yakotlus was!

As the guests arrived, they were greeted with their full titles and seated according to their rank. Members of Chief Yakotlus's kinship group performed songs and dances for the guests and told stories. Then the feasting began. No guest would leave the potlatch unsatisfied!

No guest would leave without a gift, either. Yakotlus had assembled canoes, handmade blankets, copper, furs, and many other valuable items. The first and greatest gift was presented to the highest-ranking visitor. The second and next most valuable gift went to the next in rank, and so on. As each gift was presented, a speech was made glorifying Yakotlus. The chief beamed his approval of the fine words being said about his wealth and generosity. People would remember this potlatch for years!

1. **Recognizing Words in Context**

   Find the word *show* in the passage. One definition below is a *synonym* for that word; it means the same or almost the same thing. One definition is an *antonym*; it has the opposite or nearly opposite meaning. The other has a completely different meaning. Label the definitions S for *synonym*, A for *antonym*, and D for *different*.

   _____ a. hide

   _____ b. display

   _____ c. performance

2. **Distinguishing Fact from Opinion**

   Two of the statements below present *facts*, which can be proved correct. The other statement is an *opinion*, which expresses someone's thoughts or beliefs. Label the statements F for *fact* and O for *opinion*.

   _____ a. Yakotlus was the most generous chief the Kwakiutl ever had.

   _____ b. Yakotlus gave a potlatch to celebrate his son's birth.

   _____ c. Each guest at the potlatch was given a fine gift.

3. Keeping Events in Order

Label the statements below 1, 2, and 3 to show the order in which the events happened.

_____ a. Chief Yakotlus's wife gave birth to a son.

_____ b. Members of the chief's kinship group performed for the guests.

_____ c. Speeches were made that glorified Chief Yakotlus.

4. Making Correct Inferences

Two of the statements below are correct *inferences*, or reasonable guesses. They are based on information in the passage. The other statement is an incorrect, or faulty, inference. Label the statements C for *correct* inference and F for *faulty* inference.

_____ a. The Kwakiutl showed how wealthy they were by giving things away.

_____ b. A potlatch was held every time a male child was born.

_____ c. The giving of gifts was an important part of a potlatch.

5. Understanding Main Ideas

One of the statements below expresses the main idea of the passage. One statement is too general, or too broad. The other explains only part of the passage; it is too narrow. Label the statements M for *main idea*, B for *too broad*, and N for *too narrow*.

_____ a. Yakotlus, a Kwakiutl chief, held a potlatch to celebrate the birth of a son.

_____ b. One of the richest Native American cultures was that of the people of the Pacific Northwest.

_____ c. Chief Yakotlus had assembled many fine things to give his guests.

Correct Answers, Part A _____

Correct Answers, Part B _____

Total Correct Answers _____

68

Imagine a person with all the desires and fears, thoughts and actions that make a man or a woman. Acting is becoming that imaginary person. Whether the character, or role, that the actor creates is based on someone who really lived, a playwright's concept, or a legendary being, that creation comes to life through the art of acting. Acting is an ability to react, to respond to imaginary situations and feelings. The purpose of this ancient profession, one of the world's oldest, is, as Shakespeare has Hamlet say, "to hold, as 'twere, the mirror up to Nature, to show . . . the very age and body of the Time, his form and pressure."

It is the audience that sees itself in the mirror of acting. Acting is a process of two-way communication between actor and audience. The reflection may be realistic, as the audience sees its own social behavior. The reflection may be a funny or critical exaggeration. Or the audience may see a picture of the way it thinks or a fantastic projection of the way it feels.

Acting makes use of two kinds of physical skills: movement and voice. Either may dominate. Body movement is highly developed in Far Eastern acting traditions, while the voice has ruled in Western cultures. If either voice or movement takes over completely, the activity is usually not called acting but dance, perhaps, or singing. But neither ballerinas nor operatic singers can reach the top of their professions without being able to act.

In one sense, there is no technique of acting. When the actor is on the stage or in front of a camera, there should be no thought of technique. The actor attempts simply to be there. Technique in acting has to do with getting ready to act. There are two basic requirements: developing the necessary physical external skills and freeing the internal emotional life. The physical skills needed by actors have been understood since ancient times. They are a well-developed body and voice. They include the ability to imitate other people's gestures and mannerisms. And actors need to master the physical or vocal abilities required by the type of theater.

Before the twentieth century, the inner emotional training of actors was not thought about in a systematic way. Young actors developed by watching older, more experienced performers. The creation of emotional truth on stage was largely thought of as a problem of imitation.

Reading Time _____

Recalling Facts

1. Acting is a process of two-way communication between
   - ❏ a. actor and director.
   - ❏ b. actor and audience.
   - ❏ c. actors.

2. Acting makes use of two kinds of physical skills:
   - ❏ a. movement and voice.
   - ❏ b. singing and dancing.
   - ❏ c. listening and speaking.

3. In addition to developing the necessary physical external skills, actors must
   - ❏ a. study other actors.
   - ❏ b. free the internal emotional life.
   - ❏ c. take acting lessons.

4. Acting is the ability to
   - ❏ a. project the voice.
   - ❏ b. exaggerate.
   - ❏ c. react.

5. Before the twentieth century, young actors developed by
   - ❏ a. watching more experienced performers.
   - ❏ b. reading different types of plays.
   - ❏ c. living life to the fullest.

Understanding Ideas

6. The aspect of a theater most likely to influence an actor's technique is
   - ❏ a. location.
   - ❏ b. size.
   - ❏ c. age.

7. An actor in front of a camera rather than on a stage would probably need to
   - ❏ a. become more dramatic in voice and movement.
   - ❏ b. become less dramatic in voice and movement.
   - ❏ c. react in the same way.

8. The main difference between acting now and before the twentieth century was an emphasis on
   - ❏ a. imitation rather than freed emotion.
   - ❏ b. movement rather than voice.
   - ❏ c. voice rather than movement.

9. Acting can be thought of as
   - ❏ a. a reflection of the thoughts, feelings, and actions of the actors.
   - ❏ b. a reflection of the thoughts, feelings, and actions of the audience.
   - ❏ c. a writer's interpretation of life.

10. You can conclude from the article that the most successful actors are those who
    - ❏ a. have the most experience.
    - ❏ b. study the hardest.
    - ❏ c. do not appear to be acting.

15 B   Audition

Once each year, talent scouts and officers from major theatrical, television, and motion picture companies gather in New York City to watch students from nearby acting schools audition. For the students, it is the culmination of years of hard work and study. But it is also a very nervous time for the students. At the audition, each student will have just three minutes to convince the audience that he or she is ready to become a professional actor.

To prepare for the audition, pairs of students pick scenes that showcase their strengths and talents. They work with their teachers to cut their scene to exactly three minutes—even an additional fifteen or thirty seconds can count against them. They practice endlessly in front of their classmates and teachers to shape their selection, listening to notes and suggestions and making numerous changes.

At last, they move to the space where they will actually perform. Tension mounts. Typically, students have nightmares about forgetting their lines. Finally, the day comes. They run through exercises to loosen their voices and stretch their bodies. Then, two by two, they audition before the people who can make their future—or break it—and await the outcome.

1. **Recognizing Words in Context**

   Find the word *culmination* in the passage. One definition below is a *synonym* for that word; it means the same or almost the same thing. One definition is an *antonym*; it has the opposite or nearly opposite meaning. The other has a completely different meaning. Label the definitions S for *synonym*, A for *antonym*, and D for *different*.

   _____ a. beginning

   _____ b. climax

   _____ c. crisis

2. **Distinguishing Fact from Opinion**

   Two of the statements below present *facts*, which can be proved correct. The other statement is an *opinion*, which expresses someone's thoughts or beliefs. Label the statements F for *fact* and O for *opinion*.

   _____ a. Student auditions last exactly three minutes.

   _____ b. Students audition before professional talent scouts.

   _____ c. The students feel nervous.

3. Keeping Events in Order

Label the statements below 1, 2, and 3 to show the order in which the events happened.

_____ a. The students audition before their audience of professionals.

_____ b. Talent scouts come to watch the student auditions.

_____ c. Students prepare their scenes with the help of their teachers.

4. Making Correct Inferences

Two of the statements below are correct *inferences,* or reasonable guesses. They are based on information in the passage. The other statement is an incorrect, or faulty, inference. Label the statements C for *correct* inference and F for *faulty* inference.

_____ a. A good audition can help to launch a student's career.

_____ b. The auditions are not important to the students' future.

_____ c. Acting students work long and hard to prepare for their auditions.

5. Understanding Main Ideas

One of the statements below expresses the main idea of the passage. One statement is too general, or too broad. The other explains only part of the passage; it is too narrow. Label the statements M for *main idea,* B for *too broad,* and N for *too narrow.*

_____ a. Acting school ends with an audition.

_____ b. Talent scouts and officers from television, movies, and the theater audition acting students.

_____ c. Acting students' years of preparation and study conclude with a professional three-minute audition.

Correct Answers, Part A _____

Correct Answers, Part B _____

Total Correct Answers _____

16 A   An Ancient Empire

Ethiopia has historically been an empire, expanding in area and incorporating new groups into the population. A major expansion of the empire in the second half of the nineteenth century incorporated new peoples in the west, south, and east. The result is a population of great diversity.

Various religions are represented, with numerous people following Christianity, Islam, and traditional sects. Christianity was introduced into Ethiopia in the fourth century. It was the official state religion until 1974. Although there is often a great mix of religions in any given place, Christians tend to be the most numerous in highland areas. Muslims inhabit the lowlands. Traditional religious groups are found in the south and west.

According to estimates, the national population is about 54 million. It is most densely concentrated in the highland areas. Almost 90 percent of the people live outside cities. More than 45 percent of the people are 15 years of age and younger. Both birth and death rates are high. The average life expectancy at birth is about 45 years for males and 49 years for females, among the world's lowest.

The Ethiopian economy is one of poverty. Average annual incomes are estimated at between 100 and 150 dollars per person in United States dollars. Little is produced that is not needed within the country. Most people work as farmers or herders. Traditionally, farmers have worked small, scattered plots and have low harvests. Until 1974, most Ethiopians worked the land as tenants, as members of a community, or as private owners. The government officially took ownership of all land in 1975. All farming families were allotted a parcel of land, but they did not own it nor could they sell it. Throughout most of Ethiopia, there is mixed farming, the raising of both plants and animals. In most areas, the major crops include grains. In the southern half of the country, an additional main crop is ensete, a bananalike plant whose starchy stem is eaten rather than the fruit. Animals raised include cattle, sheep, goats, donkeys, mules, horses, camels, and chickens.

There are some areas with large commercial farms. Their products go largely to Ethiopian urban markets or international trade. When the government took the land, these farms were converted to collective, or state, farms. Their significant crops include sugar cane, cotton, and fruits from the north. Sesame, sorghum, and grains are grown in the south.

Reading Time _____

Recalling Facts

1. Until 1974, the official state religion in Ethiopia was
   - ❏ a. Christianity.
   - ❏ b. Judaism.
   - ❏ c. Islam.

2. Most of the people in Ethiopia live
   - ❏ a. in lowland areas.
   - ❏ b. in cities.
   - ❏ c. outside cities.

3. The average life expectancy in Ethiopia is
   - ❏ a. among the world's highest.
   - ❏ b. the world's lowest.
   - ❏ c. among the world's lowest.

4. All land in Ethiopia is owned by
   - ❏ a. large corporations.
   - ❏ b. the government.
   - ❏ c. private owners.

5. Average annual income per person in Ethiopia is
   - ❏ a. under 150 dollars.
   - ❏ b. between 150 and 200 dollars.
   - ❏ c. about 250 dollars.

Understanding Ideas

6. Life expectancy in Ethiopia is under 50 years of age, which suggests that
   - ❏ a. most Ethiopians die of old age.
   - ❏ b. living conditions are poor.
   - ❏ c. there is a food shortage.

7. The government in Ethiopia could be described as
   - ❏ a. powerful.
   - ❏ b. democratic.
   - ❏ c. weak.

8. Ethiopia needs most of what it produces, which suggests that
   - ❏ a. Ethiopia is a center of international trade.
   - ❏ b. imports exceed exports.
   - ❏ c. exports exceed imports.

9. It is likely that the education level of the typical Ethiopian is
   - ❏ a. high.
   - ❏ b. low.
   - ❏ c. average.

10. You can conclude from the article that industry in Ethiopia is
    - ❏ a. highly developed.
    - ❏ b. a low priority.
    - ❏ c. probably minimal.

For many centuries, Ethiopia was ruled by a royal family that traced its roots to ancient Biblical times. Then the country was called Sheba and was ruled by a strong queen. According to tradition, the queen of Sheba heard that King Solomon of Jerusalem was exceptionally wise and powerful. Deciding to see for herself, she assembled a great train of camels bearing gold, jewels, and spices and set out for Jerusalem. Never had the people of Jerusalem seen such a vast parade of wealth as the queen brought into their city.

The queen had many questions with which to test King Solomon's wisdom, but his wise answers soon earned him her respect. She praised his great sagacity and goodness and gave him all the gold, jewels, and spices she had brought with her as a token of her esteem.

King Solomon fell in love with the queen of Sheba and she with him. She bore him a son, Menelik. Menelik succeeded his mother on the throne of Ethiopia and became a wise and famous ruler. He founded the imperial line of the Lion of Judah, which ruled the country in unbroken succession until 1974. Then revolution overthrew Haile Selassie, the two hundred twenty-fifth emperor to trace his lineage to the queen of Sheba.

1. **Recognizing Words in Context**

    Find the word *sagacity* in the passage. One definition below is a *synonym* for that word; it means the same or almost the same thing. One definition is an *antonym;* it has the opposite or nearly opposite meaning. The other has a completely different meaning. Label the definitions S for *synonym*, A for *antonym*, and D for *different*.

    _____ a. foolishness

    _____ b. wisdom

    _____ c. strength

2. **Distinguishing Fact from Opinion**

    Two of the statements below present *facts*, which can be proved correct. The other statement is an *opinion*, which expresses someone's thoughts or beliefs. Label the statements F for *fact* and O for *opinion*.

    _____ a. Haile Selassie was the two hundred twenty-fifth emperor of Ethiopia.

    _____ b. The queen of Sheba met with King Solomon.

    _____ c. The king's wise answers won the queen's respect.

3. Keeping Events in Order

Label the statements below 1, 2, and 3 to show the order in which the events happened.

_____ a. The queen traveled to Jerusalem with jewels and spices.

_____ b. The queen tested King Solomon with questions.

_____ c. The queen had a son by King Solomon.

4. Making Correct Inferences

Two of the statements below are correct *inferences*, or reasonable guesses. They are based on information in the passage. The other statement is an incorrect, or faulty, inference. Label the statements C for *correct* inference and F for *faulty* inference.

_____ a. Ethiopia was once a rich country.

_____ b. Sheba was once more powerful than Jerusalem.

_____ c. Ethiopia has a long and proud history.

5. Understanding Main Ideas

One of the statements below expresses the main idea of the passage. One statement is too general, or too broad. The other explains only part of the passage; it is too narrow. Label the statements M for *main idea,* B for *too broad,* and N for *too narrow.*

_____ a. Powerful kings and queens once ruled Africa.

_____ b. The people of Jerusalem were enormously impressed with the wealth of the queen of Sheba.

_____ c. Ethiopian rulers traced their beginnings to the meeting of the queen of Sheba and King Solomon of Jerusalem.

Correct Answers, Part A _____

Correct Answers, Part B _____

Total Correct Answers _____

17　A　Human Disease

A disease is a condition that impairs the proper function of the body or of one of its parts. Every living thing, both plants and animals, can yield to disease. People, for example, are often infected by tiny bacteria. And bacteria, in turn, can be infected by even more smaller viruses.

There are hundreds of different diseases. Each has its own particular set of symptoms or signs. These are clues that enable a doctor to diagnose the problem. A symptom is something a patient can detect, such as fever, bleeding, or pain. A sign is something a doctor can detect, such as a swollen blood vessel or an enlarged internal body organ.

Every disease has a cause. However, the causes of some diseases remain to be discovered. Every disease also displays a cycle of beginning, course, and end, when it disappears or it partially disables or kills its victim.

Infectious diseases can be transmitted in many ways. They can be spread in droplets through the air when infected persons sneeze or cough. Whoever inhales the droplets can become infected. Some diseases can be passed through contaminated eating or drinking utensils. Once an infectious organism gains a foothold in the body, it begins to thrive and multiply. Its progress may be slow or fast, depending upon the nature of the pathogen. The symptoms of the common cold appear within a few days of infection. But the symptoms of kuru, an uncommon disease of the nervous system, often appear three years or longer after infection.

Every infectious disease has an incubation period. This is the length of time between the pathogen's gaining a foothold in the body and the appearance of the first symptoms of the disease. Several factors also determine whether a person will become the victim of a disease after being infected. The number of invading germs in the dose of the infection influences the outbreak of disease. So does the virulence of the pathogens; that is, their power to do harm. In addition, the condition of the body's immunological defenses also affects the probability of catching a disease.

A great many infectious diseases are contagious; that is, they can easily be passed between people. To acquire certain contagious diseases, someone need only be in the presence of someone with the disease, come in contact with an infected part of the body, or eat or drink from contaminated utensils.

Reading Time _____

Recalling Facts

1. Disease strikes
   - ❏ a. mostly plants.
   - ❏ b. mostly animals.
   - ❏ c. both plants and animals.

2. Pain is
   - ❏ a. the cause of a disease.
   - ❏ b. an infection.
   - ❏ c. a symptom of a problem.

3. The symptoms of a cold appear
   - ❏ a. seconds after infection.
   - ❏ b. within a few days of infection.
   - ❏ c. weeks after infection.

4. The time between infection and the appearance of the first symptoms of a disease is the
   - ❏ a. incubation period.
   - ❏ b. contagious period.
   - ❏ c. cycle period.

5. Contagious diseases are
   - ❏ a. difficult to pass between people.
   - ❏ b. easily passed between people.
   - ❏ c. never passed between people.

Understanding Ideas

6. A person who is weak and undernourished is
   - ❏ a. more likely to yield to disease.
   - ❏ b. less likely to yield to disease.
   - ❏ c. neither more nor less likely to yield to disease.

7. A doctor's ability to detect a disease is dependent on
   - ❏ a. the cause of the disease.
   - ❏ b. the skill of the doctor.
   - ❏ c. a disease's incubation period.

8. One way to avoid a disease is to
   - ❏ a. avoid people who are infected with the disease.
   - ❏ b. avoid seeing a doctor.
   - ❏ c. understand the symptoms of the disease.

9. Diseases are caused by
   - ❏ a. impaired body function.
   - ❏ b. excessive bleeding.
   - ❏ c. bacteria and viruses.

10. You can conclude from the article that a disease with a long incubation period
    - ❏ a. has a better chance of spreading infection.
    - ❏ b. has a lesser chance of spreading infection.
    - ❏ c. will most likely prove harmless.

"Bring out your dead! Bring out your dead!" The wheels of the dead-cart rattled over the cobblestones outside the house. Molly trembled as she lay in bed next to her sister Meg. That summer of 1666, the plague held London in its grip. Each night the dead-cart rolled through the city, picking up the bodies of people who had died of the dread disease.

Molly heard her father get out of bed. Then she heard him groan and the creak of the bed as he lay back down. "Seth?" Molly heard her mother whisper. "Are you well, Seth?" Then came her father's reply. "No, Bess. I am not well."

"Molly!" her mother called. Molly got out of bed and ran to her mother. "You must take Meg and go to my sister Nell's house," Bess told her.

"Is it the plague, Mother?" Molly asked.

"Let us pray it is not," her mother said. "I will send for the doctor. You must go now, before he comes. If it is the plague, the watchmen will seal up the house with us inside. You will never get out then. I must stay with your father."

Holding her little sister's hand, Molly hurried through the dark streets. She tried to believe that it was not the plague, that her father would get well. Only time would tell.

1. Recognizing Words in Context

Find the word *well* in the passage. One definition below is a *synonym* for that word; it means the same or almost the same thing. One definition is an *antonym;* it has the opposite or nearly opposite meaning. The other has a completely different meaning. Label the definitions S for *synonym,* A for *antonym,* and D for *different.*

_____ a. sick

_____ b. satisfactorily

_____ c. healthy

2. Distinguishing Fact from Opinion

Two of the statements below present *facts,* which can be proved correct. The other statement is an *opinion,* which expresses someone's thoughts or beliefs. Label the statements F for *fact* and O for *opinion.*

_____ a. In 1666, the plague killed many people in London.

_____ b. The 1600s were a terrible time in which to live.

_____ c. The dead-cart rolled through the city at night, picking up the bodies of people who had died.

3. Keeping Events in Order

Two of the statements below describe events that happened at the same time. The other statement describes an event that happened before or after those events. Label them S for *same time*, B for *before*, and A for *after*.

_____ a. Molly heard her father say, "No, Bess. I am not well."

_____ b. The dead-cart rattled over the cobblestones outside Molly's home.

_____ c. Molly lay in bed trembling.

4. Making Correct Inferences

Two of the statements below are correct *inferences*, or reasonable guesses. They are based on information in the passage. The other statement is an incorrect, or faulty, inference. Label the statements C for *correct* inference and F for *faulty* inference.

_____ a. The plague was a highly contagious disease.

_____ b. There was no cure for the plague in those days.

_____ c. Everyone who got the plague died.

5. Understanding Main Ideas

One of the statements below expresses the main idea of the passage. One statement is too general, or too broad. The other explains only part of the passage; it is too narrow. Label the statements M for *main idea*, B for *too broad*, and N for *too narrow*.

_____ a. In 1666, the plague held London in its grip.

_____ b. Molly, a girl who lived in London in 1666, was afraid her father had the plague.

_____ c. Bubonic plague ravaged western Europe during the fourteenth century and throughout the Middle Ages.

Correct Answers, Part A _____

Correct Answers, Part B _____

Total Correct Answers _____

From prehistoric times, the Alps have been the site of human habitation. German cultures generally developed in the eastern Alps. Roman culture influenced the West. The main language groups that survive today are German, French, and Italian. Romansh, an ancient Latin language, is spoken in a region of eastern Switzerland.

Some Alpine folk traditions are still preserved and often displayed as part of the tourist and entertainment industry. Alpine music, poetry, dance, woodcarving, and embroidery are quite distinctive. Yodeling, a kind of singing, is marked by rapid switching of the voice to and from falsetto. The alpenhorn, used for signaling between valleys, is a trumpetlike wooden instrument 5 to 14 feet (1.5 to 4 meters) long.

During the first five centuries of the Christian era, Rome dominated the Alps. The Romans built roads through the passes north and west to promote trade and link their Mediterranean and northern provinces. Economic activity of the period included wine grape culture, iron-ore mining, and pottery manufacture.

Alpine valleys and many mountainsides were cleared of forests during the Middle Ages. Farmers settled the land, planted crops, and developed transhumance. In this Alpine practice, cattle are stall-fed in the villages during the winter and led to high mountain meadows for summer grazing. While the animals are gone, the farm family tends hay, grain, and other forage crops for use in the winter. Milk produced in the summer usually is made into cheese. In the winter, it is sold to dairies. Forestry is practiced in the Alps, and forest conservation programs have been developed.

During the nineteenth century, railroads were constructed, opening up the area. Hydroelectricity was developed. The electric power made by damming Alpine rivers encouraged manufacturing. The region has no coal or oil. Industrial growth caused many people to leave agriculture and take factory jobs. Types of light manufacturing, from watches to precision machinery, have thrived in the Alps.

Tourism has become a major Alpine industry. Europe has prospered as air, auto, and rail transportation to the Alps improved. One of the world's longest auto tunnels, passing through Mont Blanc, was opened in 1965. Railroads follow paths along traditional routes and passes. Winter sports gained mass popularity as a result of the accessibility of the Alpine region. Today entire villages lodge, feed, and entertain tourists. Resorts such as Innsbruck, Grenoble, and St. Moritz are world famous. All of them have hosted Olympic winter games.

Reading Time _____

Recalling Facts

1. Romansh is
   - ❑ a. a type of German food.
   - ❑ b. an ancient Latin language.
   - ❑ c. an Alpine folk tradition.

2. A trumpetlike wooden instrument used for signaling in the Alps is called the
   - ❑ a. yodel.
   - ❑ b. glockenspiel.
   - ❑ c. alpenhorn.

3. One of the world's longest auto tunnels passes through
   - ❑ a. Innsbruck.
   - ❑ b. St. Moritz.
   - ❑ c. Mont Blanc.

4. In the Alps, tourism is
   - ❑ a. a major industry.
   - ❑ b. practically nonexistent.
   - ❑ c. the result of increased manufacturing.

5. Innsbruck, Grenoble, and St. Moritz are
   - ❑ a. farming centers.
   - ❑ b. former hosts of the Olympic winter games.
   - ❑ c. the world's tallest mountains.

Understanding Ideas

6. The Alpine region can be characterized as
   - ❑ a. a commercial center.
   - ❑ b. prosperous.
   - ❑ c. economically deprived.

7. Farming in the Alps is primarily
   - ❑ a. run by big businesses.
   - ❑ b. a family business.
   - ❑ c. a seasonal job.

8. You can conclude from the article that transhumance was developed as a result of
   - ❑ a. limited winter grazing for cattle.
   - ❑ b. an increase in the cattle population.
   - ❑ c. laws regarding the humane treatment of animals.

9. It is likely that the Alpine region would not have prospered without
   - ❑ a. the many improvements in transportation.
   - ❑ b. forest conservation.
   - ❑ c. the skiing industry.

10. You can conclude from the article that resorts in the Alpine region were chosen to host the Olympic winter games because
    - ❑ a. they are well-known to tourists.
    - ❑ b. Alpine folk traditions are preserved there.
    - ❑ c. of their ideal conditions for winter sports.

18 B The Iceman

In the summer of 1991, hikers on an Alpine glacier came across the body of a man frozen in the ice. They contacted the authorities, who came to exhume the body. The team retrieving the body guessed that it must be very old, but they did not know it was one of the most important archaeological finds of the century.

The body, whom they named the Iceman, was flown to Innsbruck, Austria, for examination. There, scientists determined that the man was as much as 5,300 years old, the oldest preserved human body ever found.

What was the Iceman doing when he died? Researchers think he may have been a shepherd, grazing his flock when a storm struck. Or perhaps he was a hunter who had gone to the valley to cut wood for a new bow. Perhaps he had curled up in a trench to wait out the storm, fell asleep, and froze to death. Or he may have been in search of food when the storm overtook him.

Scientists continue to study the man who died more than five hundred centuries ago for what he can tell us about how people lived in a time when metal was just beginning to replace stone for tools and utensils.

1. **Recognizing Words in Context**

   Find the word *exhume* in the passage. One definition below is a *synonym* for that word; it means the same or almost the same thing. One definition is an *antonym;* it has the opposite or nearly opposite meaning. The other has a completely different meaning. Label the definitions S for *synonym*, A for *antonym*, and D for *different*.

   _____ a. raise

   _____ b. cover

   _____ c. claim

2. **Distinguishing Fact from Opinion**

   Two of the statements below present *facts,* which can be proved correct. The other statement is an *opinion,* which expresses someone's thoughts or beliefs. Label the statements F for *fact* and O for *opinion*.

   _____ a. Scientists continue to study the Iceman's body.

   _____ b. The Iceman was one of the most important archaeological finds of the century.

   _____ c. The Iceman was found in the summer of 1991.

3. Keeping Events in Order

Label the statements below 1, 2, and 3 to show the order in which the events happened.

_____ a. The body was flown to Innsbruck for examination.

_____ b. Hikers found the frozen body of a man.

_____ c. Scientists decided the body was over 5,000 years old.

4. Making Correct Inferences

Two of the statements below are correct *inferences*, or reasonable guesses. They are based on information in the passage. The other statement is an incorrect, or faulty, inference. Label the statements C for *correct* inference and F for *faulty* inference.

_____ a. The Iceman is important mainly as a curiosity.

_____ b. The Iceman is a link with the ancient past.

_____ c. The Iceman can tell us much about how people lived 5,000 years ago.

5. Understanding Main Ideas

One of the statements below expresses the main idea of the passage. One statement is too general, or too broad. The other explains only part of the passage; it is too narrow. Label the statements M for *main idea,* B for *too broad,* and N for *too narrow.*

_____ a. Researchers believe the Iceman may have been a shepherd or a hunter who died in a storm.

_____ b. A man's body preserved in Alpine ice provides important clues to how ancient people lived.

_____ c. The Iceman is a body found frozen in the Alps.

Correct Answers, Part A _____

Correct Answers, Part B _____

Total Correct Answers _____

Anne Hutchinson, Religious Pioneer

Anne Hutchinson was one of the first New England colonists to challenge the authority of the Puritan leaders in religious matters. She preferred following her conscience over blind obedience. Her protest helped establish the principle of freedom of religion.

Anne Marbury was born in Alford, England, and baptized on July 20, 1591. Her father, an English clergyman, was twice imprisoned for preaching against the established Church of England. Although Marbury had no formal education, she learned much by listening to her father and his friends discuss religion and government. When Marbury was 14, her father was appointed to St. Martin's Church in London. At 21, she married William Hutchinson, her childhood sweetheart, and they returned to Alford to live. They had 14 children. Despite her busy household, Hutchinson was active in religious affairs and often made the 24-mile (39-kilometer) journey to Boston, England, to hear John Cotton preach. In 1633, Cotton was compelled to leave England because of his Puritan sympathies. With Hutchinson's eldest son, Edward, he fled to New England. The Hutchinsons, with their other children, followed the next year and settled in Boston, Massachusetts.

Soon Hutchinson was holding weekly prayer meetings for the women of the colony. At these meetings, she often criticized the preaching of the clergy. She believed that the Lord dwelt within each individual, and she proclaimed that faith solely would attain salvation. This was in opposition to the teachings of the Puritan leaders. By 1636, she had recruited many converts, including her brother-in-law, the Reverend John Wheelwright, and the young governor, Henry Vane. John Cotton initially supported her but later publicly renounced her teachings.

With Governor Vane a convert, the other leaders feared civil disobedience and sought to regain control. When Vane returned to England in 1636, they obtained the governorship for John Winthrop. He banished Wheelwright to New Hampshire and brought Hutchinson to trial. She was banished in November 1637, but because of ill health was permitted to spend the winter in nearby Roxbury.

During the winter, Cotton and other clergy pressured Hutchinson to deny her beliefs. When she refused, she was excommunicated from the church. She and her family and friends moved to Rhode Island in 1638 and founded a new colony. After her husband's death in 1642, Hutchinson moved with her younger children to Pelham Bay in New York. In 1643, she and most of her family were killed by Native Americans.

Reading Time _____

Recalling Facts

1. Anne Hutchinson believed in
   - ❏ a. women's liberation.
   - ❏ b. religious freedom.
   - ❏ c. a strong central government.

2. Anne Hutchinson's father was
   - ❏ a. a teacher.
   - ❏ b. a politician.
   - ❏ c. a clergyman.

3. Anne Hutchinson believed that in order to attain salvation, people had to
   - ❏ a. follow the laws of the church.
   - ❏ b. have faith.
   - ❏ c. move to New England.

4. Originally, Anne Hutchinson was a follower of
   - ❏ a. John Cotton's Puritan beliefs.
   - ❏ b. the Church of England.
   - ❏ c. John Calvin.

5. As a result of her religious beliefs, Anne Hutchinson was
   - ❏ a. burned at the stake.
   - ❏ b. banished to a foreign country.
   - ❏ c. excommunicated from the church.

Understanding Ideas

6. It is likely that Anne Hutchinson's religious ideas were
   - ❏ a. very popular in England.
   - ❏ b. influenced by those of her father.
   - ❏ c. a result of her formal education.

7. You can conclude from the article that during Anne Hutchinson's time, women
   - ❏ a. were unlikely to be religious leaders.
   - ❏ b. often spoke out about their religious beliefs.
   - ❏ c. were against religious freedom.

8. You can conclude from the article that during Anne Hutchinson's time, freedom of religion
   - ❏ a. was not encouraged.
   - ❏ b. was tolerated.
   - ❏ c. was allowed only in New England.

9. Anne Hutchinson was most likely a
   - ❏ a. poor teacher.
   - ❏ b. misguided fanatic.
   - ❏ c. convincing speaker.

10. If Anne Hutchinson were alive today, it is likely that
   - ❏ a. her religious beliefs would be accepted.
   - ❏ b. she would be banished from the United States.
   - ❏ c. she would be elected to public office.

19   B   The Trials of Anne Hutchinson

Pregnant and ill, Anne Hutchinson stood before her accusers. "Pray let me sit, gentlemen," she begged. The men sitting before her in judgment refused her request. Hutchinson had defied both the church leaders and the government. For this, she was put on trial twice. In this first trial, the government was trying her for challenging its authority. The Reverend John Wheelwright, Hutchinson's brother-in-law, had already been tried for contempt and sedition—inciting people to resist lawful authority. Found guilty, he had been expelled from the Massachusetts Bay Colony. Now it was Anne's turn.

At last, seeing that Anne was on the verge of collapse under the bitter attacks, the court let her sit. There was no doubt of the outcome of this trial—Anne Hutchinson was guilty as charged.

Hutchinson's second trial was for heresy—holding opinions contrary to those of the church. Ill as she was, Anne challenged her questioners with her expert knowledge of the Bible and remarkable speaking ability. The weeks of questioning wore her down, however. To end her ordeal, Anne repented, but this did not satisfy the church leaders. They said, "Her repentance is not in her countenance." Anne Hutchinson was banished from the colony.

1. **Recognizing Words in Context**

   Find the word *bitter* in the passage. One definition below is a *synonym* for that word; it means the same or almost the same thing. One definition is an *antonym;* it has the opposite or nearly opposite meaning. The other has a completely different meaning. Label the definitions S for *synonym,* A for *antonym,* and D for *different.*

   _____ a. bad-tasting

   _____ b. gentle

   _____ c. harsh

2. **Distinguishing Fact from Opinion**

   Two of the statements below present *facts,* which can be proved correct. The other statement is an *opinion,* which expresses someone's thoughts or beliefs. Label the statements F for *fact* and O for *opinion.*

   _____ a. Anne Hutchinson was pregnant and ill at the time of her trials.

   _____ b. Hutchinson's accusers would not let her sit until she was on the verge of collapse.

   _____ c. Hutchinson's accusers were cruel and unfeeling men.

3. Keeping Events in Order

Label the statements below 1, 2, and 3 to show the order in which the events happened.

_____ a. Anne Hutchinson was tried by the church leaders for heresy.

_____ b. Anne Hutchinson was tried by the government for challenging its authority.

_____ c. Anne Hutchinson was banished from the colony.

4. Making Correct Inferences

Two of the statements below are correct *inferences*, or reasonable guesses. They are based on information in the passage. The other statement is an incorrect, or faulty, inference. Label the statements C for *correct* inference and F for *faulty* inference.

_____ a. No matter what Anne Hutchinson said at her trials, she would have been found guilty.

_____ b. In Hutchinson's time, the government and the church were closely connected.

_____ c. When Anne Hutchinson repented, she did so because she knew she was wrong.

5. Understanding Main Ideas

One of the statements below expresses the main idea of the passage. One statement is too general, or too broad. The other explains only part of the passage; it is too narrow. Label the statements M for *main idea*, B for *too broad*, and N for *too narrow*.

_____ a. Anne Hutchinson was tried by both the government and the church for defying their authority, found guilty, and banished.

_____ b. There was no separation of church and state in the Massachusetts Bay Colony.

_____ c. The church leaders accused Anne Hutchinson of heresy.

Correct Answers, Part A _____

Correct Answers, Part B _____

Total Correct Answers _____

Painting and power shovels, sonatas and submarines, dramas and dynamos—they all have one thing in common. They are fashioned by people. They are artificial, in contrast to everything that is natural—plants, animals, minerals. The average modern-day person would classify paintings, sonatas, and dramas as forms of art, while viewing power shovels, submarines, and dynamos as products of technology. This distinction, however, is a modern one that dates from an eighteenth-century point of view.

In earlier times, the word *art* referred to any useful skill. Shoemaking, metalworking, medicine, agriculture, and even warfare were all once classified as arts. They were equated with what are today called the fine arts—painting, sculpture, music, architecture, literature, dance, and related fields. In that broader sense, art has been defined as a skill in making or doing, based on true and adequate reasoning.

The earlier and more comprehensive understanding of art can be seen in the Latin and Greek words that were used to describe it. The Latin word *ars* was applied to any skill or knowledge that was needed to produce something. From it, the English word *art* is derived, as is the word *artificial*, which describes something produced by a human being. The Greek word is even more revealing. It is *techne*, the source for the term *technology*, which most people would never confuse with art.

The liberal arts originated in ancient Greek and Roman attitudes toward different types of skills. The Greek philosophers, primarily Plato and Aristotle, did not separate the fine arts from the so-called useful arts, as is done today. They distinguished between the liberal arts and the servile arts. Fine arts were classified among the labors of the lower classes in ancient Greece or Rome. The word *liberal* comes from Latin and means "suitable for a freeman." Studies that were taken up by free citizens were thus regarded as the liberal arts. They were arts that required superior mental ability—logic or astronomy, for example. Such arts were in contrast to skills that were basically labor.

The Latin word for *servile* was used to describe the handiwork that was often done by slaves, or at least by members of the lower classes. The servile arts involved such skills as metalworking, painting, sculpture, or shoemaking. The products of these arts provided material comforts and conveniences. But such arts were not themselves considered to be beautiful or noble.

Reading Time _____

Recalling Facts

1. In earlier times, *art* referred to
   - ❏ a. any useful skill.
   - ❏ b. only to sculpture and painting.
   - ❏ c. only to agriculture and warfare.

2. Today people view power shovels, submarines, and dynamos as
   - ❏ a. forms of art.
   - ❏ b. products of technology.
   - ❏ c. trappings of civilization.

3. In earlier times, shoemaking was considered
   - ❏ a. a profession.
   - ❏ b. a trade.
   - ❏ c. an art.

4. According to the Romans, logic and astronomy required
   - ❏ a. a liberal education.
   - ❏ b. thoughtful insight.
   - ❏ c. superior mental ability.

5. To the Romans, *liberal* meant
   - ❏ a. produced by a human being.
   - ❏ b. suitable for a freeman.
   - ❏ c. work done by the lower classes.

Understanding Ideas

6. The article suggests that art
   - ❏ a. has had many different interpretations.
   - ❏ b. is to be enjoyed for itself.
   - ❏ c. was ignored by the Greeks and Romans.

7. One thing products of art and technology have in common is
   - ❏ a. a human origin.
   - ❏ b. an origin in nature.
   - ❏ c. a classification as fine arts.

8. Greek and Roman attitudes toward the arts
   - ❏ a. were never fully recorded.
   - ❏ b. parallel people's attitudes today.
   - ❏ c. are different from people's attitudes today.

9. References in the article to the Greeks and Romans suggest that art
   - ❏ a. had its foundations in Greece.
   - ❏ b. is an ancient concept.
   - ❏ c. was relatively unknown to them.

10. To the Romans, products of the servile arts were seen as
    - ❏ a. decorative.
    - ❏ b. functional.
    - ❏ c. noble.

Leonardo da Vinci (1452–1519), like many people of his time, dreamed of flying. He spent years observing birds in flight and sketching them. His notebooks contain drawing after drawing of birds with outstretched wings. Leonardo tried to solve the mystery. How did a bird's wings hold it aloft? How did they enable the bird to soar, to turn, to dive?

Leonardo sought to turn his dream into reality. He designed batlike wings made of wooden ribs with fabric stretched across them. The wings of one of his early flying machines were hooked up to a hand crank. When the crank was turned, the wings flapped. A later design used a system of stirrups and pulleys so that the flier could flap the wings by pedaling.

Some inventors tried to fly by strapping wings to their backs and jumping off high towers. Did Leonardo do that? No one knows. Leonardo believed that his machine would work and would "fill the world with its great fame." Someone who lived at the same time, though, wrote that "Leonardo da Vinci also tried to fly, but he, too, failed." The writer added, "He was a magnificent painter." Nevertheless, more than 300 years before flying machines were perfected, Leonardo sketched plans for prototypes of an airplane and a helicopter.

1. **Recognizing Words in Context**

Find the word *hooked* in the passage. One definition below is a *synonym* for that word; it means the same or almost the same thing. One definition is an *antonym*; it has the opposite or nearly opposite meaning. The other has a completely different meaning. Label the definitions S for *synonym*, A for *antonym*, and D for *different*.

_____ a. unattached

_____ b. caught

_____ c. joined

2. **Distinguishing Fact from Opinion**

Two of the statements below present *facts*, which can be proved correct. The other statement is an *opinion*, which expresses someone's thoughts or beliefs. Label the statements F for *fact* and O for *opinion*.

_____ a. Leonardo designed batlike wings made of wooden ribs with fabric stretched across them.

_____ b. Some men tried to fly by strapping wings to their backs and jumping off high towers.

_____ c. Leonardo da Vinci was a magnificent painter.

3. Keeping Events in Order

Label the statements below 1, 2, and 3 to show the order in which the events happened.

_____ a. The wings of one of his early flying machines were hooked up to a hand crank.

_____ b. Leonardo da Vinci spent years observing birds in flight and sketching them.

_____ c. A later design used a system of stirrups and pulleys so that the flier could flap the wings by pedaling.

4. Making Correct Inferences

Two of the statements below are correct *inferences,* or reasonable guesses. They are based on information in the passage. The other statement is an incorrect, or faulty, inference. Label the statements C for *correct* inference and F for *faulty* inference.

_____ a. Leonardo da Vinci was both an artist and an engineer.

_____ b. Leonardo was a methodical person.

_____ c. Leonardo was a better painter than an engineer.

5. Understanding Main Ideas

One of the statements below expresses the main idea of the passage. One statement is too general, or too broad. The other explains only part of the passage; it is too narrow. Label the statements M for *main idea,* B for *too broad,* and N for *too narrow.*

_____ a. Leonardo da Vinci sketched birds in flight.

_____ b. The history of people's attempts to fly goes back many centuries.

_____ c. Leonardo da Vinci tried to turn his dream of flying into reality.

Correct Answers, Part A _____

Correct Answers, Part B _____

Total Correct Answers _____

The sudden shaking of the ground that occurs when masses of rock change position below the Earth's surface is called an earthquake. The shifting masses send out shock waves that may be powerful enough to alter the surface of the Earth. They may thrust up cliffs and open great cracks in the ground.

Earthquakes occur almost continuously. Fortunately, most of them can be detected only by sensitive instruments called seismographs. Others are felt as small tremors. Some, however, cause major catastrophes. They produce such tragic and dramatic effects as destroyed cities, broken dams, earth slides, giant sea waves, and volcanic eruptions. A very great earthquake usually occurs at least once a year somewhere in the world.

On the average, about 10,000 people die each year as a result of earthquakes. According to a study carried out by the United Nations and covering the years 1926 to 1950, earthquakes caused 350,000 deaths, and property damage losses exceeded 10 billion dollars. As cities expand for a rapidly increasing world population, it is likely that there will be even greater losses of life and property, in spite of improved methods of detection and better warning systems. People have long been concerned about earthquake hazards. The oldest chronicle comes from the Chinese more than 3,000 years ago.

Although it is certain that violent Earth tremors in themselves are destructive, there are often other kinds of Earth movements that are triggered by earthquake shock waves. The violent shaking that accompanies many earthquakes often causes rock slides, snow avalanches, and landslides. In some areas, these events are frequently more devastating than the Earth tremor itself.

Floods and fires are also caused by earthquakes. Floods can arise from the giant sea waves earthquakes cause along coastlines. They can also arise from large-scale disturbances in enclosed bodies of water, such as lakes and canals, and from the failure of dams. Fire produced the greatest property loss following the 1906 San Francisco earthquake, when 521 blocks in the city burned uncontrollably for three days. Fire also followed the 1923 Tokyo earthquake, causing much damage and hardship for the citizens of that city.

Some earthquakes are associated with human activity. Dynamite or atomic explosions, for example, can sometimes cause mild quakes. The injection of liquid wastes deep into the Earth and the pressures resulting from holding vast amounts of water in reservoirs behind large dams can also trigger minor earthquakes.

Reading Time _____

Recalling Facts

1. Earthquakes occur when
   - ❑ a. volcanoes erupt and shake the Earth.
   - ❑ b. masses of rock change position below the Earth's surface.
   - ❑ c. giant sea waves hit the shore.

2. Earthquakes happen
   - ❑ a. almost continuously.
   - ❑ b. very frequently.
   - ❑ c. fairly rarely.

3. The average number of people killed by earthquakes each year is about
   - ❑ a. 1,000.
   - ❑ b. 10,000.
   - ❑ c. 100,000.

4. A very great earthquake occurs at least once
   - ❑ a. a month.
   - ❑ b. a year.
   - ❑ c. a decade.

5. Instruments that detect earthquakes are called
   - ❑ a. geographs.
   - ❑ b. rock slide monitors.
   - ❑ c. seismographs.

Understanding Ideas

6. The damage caused by an earthquake occurs
   - ❑ a. both before and during the earthquake.
   - ❑ b. both during and after the earthquake.
   - ❑ c. only after the earthquake.

7. Earthquake detection and warning systems are being improved
   - ❑ a. because they can help prevent earthquakes.
   - ❑ b. so that they can replace seismographs.
   - ❑ c. because they can help save lives and property.

8. People have written about earthquakes
   - ❑ a. for over 5,000 years.
   - ❑ b. for almost 2,000 years.
   - ❑ c. only in the nineteenth and twentieth centuries.

9. Earthquake deaths and damages will likely increase
   - ❑ a. as cities grow larger.
   - ❑ b. as detection and warning systems are improved.
   - ❑ c. as volcanic activity increases.

10. Most earthquakes can be detected only by sensitive instruments, which suggests that
    - ❑ a. the instruments should be adjusted.
    - ❑ b. the earthquakes are very severe.
    - ❑ c. the earthquakes are too slight to be felt.

The Great San Francisco Earthquake

The evening of October 17, 1989, was warm and breezy. "Good earthquake weather," Sara Kidd thought as she left her San Francisco office. Moments later, the building began to shake. Sara watched in horror as the double-decker highway across the street collapsed onto the lower roadway, flattening cars like tin cans. All around, buildings swayed and crumpled. Roads bulged and rippled, bouncing cars around like an amusement park ride. This was no ride, though. It was the third most lethal earthquake in U.S. history.

As suddenly as it started, the shaking stopped. Sara remembered her grandfather's stories about the great San Francisco earthquake of 1906. He had been awakened by a howling noise, he said. The earth rumbled, shook, and pitched. He ran into the street just before his house fell apart, reduced to kindling. Fueled by overturned stoves, scattered blazes joined together into firestorms that roared across the city. By the time the fires died out three days later, 28,188 buildings had been destroyed, and 2,500 people had died.

The city had learned its lesson from the quake of '06: be prepared! Although the quake of '89 was costly, only about 100 people died. "I'm happy this wasn't 'The Big One,'" Sara said.

1. Recognizing Words in Context

Find the word *lethal* in the passage. One definition below is a *synonym* for that word; it means the same or almost the same thing. One definition is an *antonym;* it has the opposite or nearly opposite meaning. The other has a completely different meaning. Label the definitions S for *synonym*, A for *antonym*, and D for *different*.

_____ a. slow

_____ b. deadly

_____ c. beneficial

2. Distinguishing Fact from Opinion

Two of the statements below present *facts*, which can be proved correct. The other statement is an *opinion*, which expresses someone's thoughts or beliefs. Label the statements F for *fact* and O for *opinion*.

_____ a. Sara Kidd thought it was good earthquake weather.

_____ b. In the earthquake of 1906, 28,188 buildings were destroyed and 2,500 people died.

_____ c. The quake of 1989 was the third most lethal earthquake in United States history.

3. Keeping Events in Order

Label the statements below 1, 2, and 3 to show the order in which the events happened.

_____ a. Fueled by overturned stoves, buildings caught fire.

_____ b. Sara's grandfather's house was reduced to kindling.

_____ c. Sara's grandfather ran into the street.

4. Making Correct Inferences

Two of the statements below are correct *inferences*, or reasonable guesses. They are based on information in the passage. The other statement is an incorrect, or faulty, inference. Label the statements C for *correct* inference and F for *faulty* inference.

_____ a. No matter how prepared a city is, an earthquake can still be deadly.

_____ b. The next San Francisco earthquake will be even less deadly than the quake of 1989.

_____ c. In 1989, people were still expecting "The Big One"—San Francisco's deadliest earthquake—to happen.

5. Understanding Main Ideas

One of the statements below expresses the main idea of the passage. One statement is too general, or too broad. The other explains only part of the passage; it is too narrow. Label the statements M for *main idea,* B for *too broad,* and N for *too narrow.*

_____ a. About 100 people died in the 1989 San Francisco earthquake.

_____ b. San Francisco has survived two deadly earthquakes in the twentieth century.

_____ c. People have been experiencing earthquakes for thousands of years.

Correct Answers, Part A _____

Correct Answers, Part B _____

Total Correct Answers _____

In its simplest sense, hunger is merely a desire. You arrive home in the afternoon and head for the refrigerator, looking for something to eat. You have already had breakfast and lunch, and dinner will soon be ready, so you are not in great need of food. For millions of people on Earth, however, hunger represents a genuine need—a large-scale lack of food. This lack may be partial; there is some food, but never enough. The lack of food may also be total. A total lack of food for a whole population is called a famine—obviously related to the word *famished*. The result of famine is mass starvation, something that has often happened in world history.

A famine is defined as an extreme and long-term shortage of food. A famine can affect a whole country, or it may be regional. Warfare has been the most common historical cause of famine. It destroys not only food supplies but distribution systems as well.

There are two main causes of famine: natural and human. Natural causes include disasters such as drought, insect plagues, excessive rainfall and flooding, and unseasonably cold weather. In a large nation, such as the United States, these factors may operate to cause shortages and high prices. But they have never caused a famine, because food can be imported or carried from one part of the country to another. In a smaller, less diverse society, a natural disaster can cause extreme hardship. In Ireland, during the 1840s, the failure of the potato crop led to the deaths of at least one million people and the emigration of thousands. In ancient societies, a flood or drought could easily cause famine because there were no outside sources of food relief. Overpopulation, a kind of natural cause, has led to severe famines. Significant twentieth-century improvements in agriculture—the Green Revolution—have eased this problem considerably.

In the twentieth century, human causes of famine have been at least as prevalent as natural causes. Apart from warfare, misguided economic reform programs carried out in the name of communism and socialism have led to the deaths of millions in the Soviet Union, China, Ethiopia, and Mozambique. Farm families were driven from villages by force and herded onto collective farms. Individual initiative was abolished, and agricultural production suffered badly. Agriculture was run by government bureaucracies, with little freedom of choice for producers or consumers.

Reading Time _____

Recalling Facts

1. Famine is
   - ❏ a. a temporary lack of food.
   - ❏ b. the experience of hunger.
   - ❏ c. an extreme and long-term shortage of food.

2. The most common historical cause of famine is
   - ❏ a. warfare.
   - ❏ b. flooding.
   - ❏ c. freezing temperatures.

3. The two main causes of famine are
   - ❏ a. natural and unnatural.
   - ❏ b. natural and human.
   - ❏ c. animal and human.

4. The United States has never experienced famine because
   - ❏ a. food can be carried from one part of the country to another.
   - ❏ b. there has never been a food shortage.
   - ❏ c. the country is underpopulated.

5. A cause of famine in the Soviet Union has been
   - ❏ a. the lack of individual initiative.
   - ❏ b. misguided economic reform programs.
   - ❏ c. poor farming methods.

Understanding Ideas

6. The relationship between hunger and famine can be described as
   - ❏ a. desire versus necessity.
   - ❏ b. itch versus scratch.
   - ❏ c. presence versus absence.

7. For famine to occur, there must be a lack of food as well as
   - ❏ a. high prices.
   - ❏ b. no outside sources of food relief.
   - ❏ c. severe changes in climate.

8. The United States has avoided famine because of
   - ❏ a. a good distribution system.
   - ❏ b. good luck.
   - ❏ c. government regulations.

9. Large, diverse societies are more likely to
   - ❏ a. experience famine from natural causes.
   - ❏ b. experience famine from human causes.
   - ❏ c. avoid famine.

10. You can conclude from the article that one way to ease the problem of famine is to
    - ❏ a. encourage improvements in agriculture.
    - ❏ b. avoid economic reform programs.
    - ❏ c. demand government intervention.

Patrick O'Riordan looked with horror at his potato field. The leaves and stalks of the plants were black and slimy with fungus. The dreaded potato blight had arrived. Behind him he heard his wife cry, "Oh, no, Patrick! Whatever shall we do?"

Do? There was nothing that could be done. There would be no potato crop this year. There would be no money to pay the landlord's rent. There would be no potatoes—their family's main source of food—to keep them fed through the winter. "We'll try to stay alive, Brigid," Patrick told her. "That's what we will do."

That winter of 1846–47 was unusually severe. Patrick, Brigid, and their children huddled against the cold in their windowless mud hut. Brigid wrapped rags around her children's bare feet to protect them from the frozen ground. She stirred a pot of "soup" that hung over the fire—a soup of water, tree bark, and roots. It filled their stomachs but gave little nourishment. All of them grew thin and gaunt.

Then the landlord's agent came. "You haven't paid the rent," he told them. "You have to leave." The O'Riordans gathered up their few possessions and left their home.

"We'll go to America, Brigid," Patrick told her. "We'll start a new life there."

1. **Recognizing Words in Context**

   Find the word *cry* in the passage. One definition below is a *synonym* for that word; it means the same or almost the same thing. One definition is an *antonym*; it has the opposite or nearly opposite meaning. The other has a completely different meaning. Label the definitions S for *synonym*, A for *antonym*, and D for *different*.

   _____ a. shout

   _____ b. whisper

   _____ c. weep

2. **Distinguishing Fact from Opinion**

   Two of the statements below present *facts*, which can be proved correct. The other statement is an *opinion*, which expresses someone's thoughts or beliefs. Label the statements F for *fact* and O for *opinion*.

   _____ a. A blight destroyed potato crops in Ireland.

   _____ b. The O'Riordan family had no food.

   _____ c. The landlord's agent was cruel to throw out starving people.

3. **Keeping Events in Order**

   Label the statements below 1, 2, and 3 to show the order in which the events happened.

   _____ a. Patrick told his wife that they would go to America.

   _____ b. The leaves and stalks of the potato plants were covered with slimy black fungus.

   _____ c. The landlord's agent evicted the O'Riordan family.

4. **Making Correct Inferences**

   Two of the statements below are correct *inferences*, or reasonable guesses. They are based on information in the passage. The other statement is an incorrect, or faulty, inference. Label the statements C for *correct* inference and F for *faulty* inference.

   _____ a. Potatoes were the main source of food for Irish peasants.

   _____ b. The potato blight caused families to starve.

   _____ c. Everything would be all right when the O'Riordan family reached America.

5. **Understanding Main Ideas**

   One of the statements below expresses the main idea of the passage. One statement is too general, or too broad. The other explains only part of the passage; it is too narrow. Label the statements M for *main idea*, B for *too broad*, and N for *too narrow*.

   _____ a. The O'Riordan family, their potato crop destroyed by blight, decided to go to America.

   _____ b. During the 1840s, the failure of the potato crop led to widespread famine in Ireland.

   _____ c. Patrick's potato plants were black and slimy with fungus.

Correct Answers, Part A _____

Correct Answers, Part B _____

Total Correct Answers _____

The earliest known urban culture on the Indian subcontinent existed in the Indus Valley from about 2500 B.C. to about 1700 B.C. The earliest human settlements in the area were on the Pakistan-Iran border. They date from the late Stone Age. These settlements probably began in about 4000 B.C. The people who lived in them led a seminomadic existence. They herded animals from one place to another and grew some food.

Sometime in the third millennium, increased population led to an eastward migration to the Valley. It is a floodplain, much like the Nile region of Egypt. The annual flooding brought deposits of silt. The soil was good for growing food and other crops with a minimum of labor and tools. The first settlements were probably established near the Indus Delta in the south. Later ones developed as civilization spread north and east.

The early centuries of settlement appear to have been a time of rapid population increase. The expansion resulted, in spite of the many different settlements, in a fairly uniform culture and a strong measure of economic and political control. The civil government in the leading cities was probably under the control of a class of priests or priest-kings, as in Egypt.

The animals raised by the Indus civilization were humped cattle, buffalo, sheep, goats, pigs, camels, dogs, cats, and domestic fowl. Elephants were also in the region. They may also have been domesticated.

Excavations of the Indus cities have produced evidence of a high level of artistic activity. There are a number of stone sculptures, cast-bronze figures, and terra-cotta figurines. Most of these are unclothed females heavily laden with jewelry. A few standing males have also been discovered. The figurines probably represent gods and goddesses, but many, such as animals and carts, are toys. It appears that the only painting was that done on pottery.

The religious beliefs of the Indus society are mostly a matter of conjecture. Buildings believed to be temples have been excavated. There were also animal cults devoted to the bull, the buffalo, and the tiger. Excavations at burial sites indicate belief in an afterlife. Household goods buried with bodies suggest the hope that the individuals would later need them.

The uniform civilization of the Indus Valley came to an end in about 1700 B.C. Whether this was due to a major invasion, gradual incursion by outsiders, or other factors is unknown.

Reading Time _____

Recalling Facts

1. The earliest human settlers in the region lived
   - ❑ a. permanently in one place.
   - ❑ b. seminomadic lives.
   - ❑ c. in mud houses.

2. Most of the figurines excavated in the Indus Valley are
   - ❑ a. male.
   - ❑ b. female.
   - ❑ c. animals.

3. The religion of the Indus society
   - ❑ a. is mostly a matter of conjecture.
   - ❑ b. was probably Christian.
   - ❑ c. changed with the seasons.

4. The Indus civilization consisted of
   - ❑ a. one main settlement.
   - ❑ b. many different settlements.
   - ❑ c. nomadic tribes.

5. The end of the uniform civilization of the Indus Valley was caused by
   - ❑ a. a major invasion.
   - ❑ b. massive flooding.
   - ❑ c. unknown factors.

Understanding Ideas

6. The late Stone Age settlements that began in about 4000 B.C.
   - ❑ a. were more advanced than the Indus Valley settlements.
   - ❑ b. were established later than the Indus Valley settlements.
   - ❑ c. may have served as models for the Indus Valley settlements.

7. You can conclude from the article that religion
   - ❑ a. was not very important in the Indus civilization.
   - ❑ b. in Indus society decreased in importance as time passed.
   - ❑ c. was an important part of Indus civilization.

8. People living in the Indus Valley may have regarded painting as a
   - ❑ a. waste of time.
   - ❑ b. means of decoration.
   - ❑ c. high form of artistic expression.

9. Knowledge of the Indus civilization comes largely from
   - ❑ a. books.
   - ❑ b. archaeological digs.
   - ❑ c. cave paintings.

10. It is likely that early peoples settled in river valleys with rich soil because they
    - ❑ a. depended on crops for food.
    - ❑ b. needed special soil for building.
    - ❑ c. enjoyed living near the water.

Ravi walked quickly through the streets of MohenjoñDaro, his city of baked brick in the Indus Valley. He didn't want to be late for his martial arts lesson. Now fourteen, Ravi had been studying since he was seven. He had mastered two of the three stages of kalarippayat. Soon he would undergo testing to see if he was ready for the third stage, ankathari, or armed combat.

Over the years, Ravi had learned self-control, concentration, and humility. He had mastered his emotions and his energy. He hoped that his teacher would decide that he was ready to learn the secret science of marmas, or vital points. By aiming their blows at these vulnerable areas, masters of the art could kill an opponent instantly or leave the opponent disabled for months.

There were more than a hundred marmas, Ravi knew. Seven of them were so critical that touch was not needed. Ravi had experienced this himself. An instructor had simply pointed his index finger at one of those marmas, and Ravi had lost his balance and fallen. Another instructor had made a boy who was behaving badly lose consciousness by pointing a finger at him. Ravi was eager to advance to this stage of knowledge. He thought that he was ready. Would it be today? Ravi hoped so.

1. Recognizing Words in Context

Find the word *advance* in the passage. One definition below is a *synonym* for that word; it means the same or almost the same thing. One definition is an *antonym;* it has the opposite or nearly opposite meaning. The other has a completely different meaning. Label the definitions S for *synonym,* A for *antonym,* and D for *different.*

_____ a. proceed

_____ b. retreat

_____ c. increase

2. Distinguishing Fact from Opinion

Two of the statements below present *facts,* which can be proved correct. The other statement is an *opinion,* which expresses someone's thoughts or beliefs. Label the statements F for *fact* and O for *opinion.*

_____ a. Ravi was studying a form of martial arts.

_____ b. A master of the art could kill an opponent with a single blow.

_____ c. Ravi was ready to advance to the third stage.

3. Keeping Events in Order

Two of the statements below describe events that happened at the same time. The other statement describes an event that happened before or after those events. Label them S for *same time*, B for *before*, and A for *after*.

_____ a. An instructor pointed his index finger at Ravi.

_____ b. Ravi walked through the streets on his way to his lesson.

_____ c. Ravi lost his balance and fell.

4. Making Correct Inferences

Two of the statements below are correct *inferences*, or reasonable guesses. They are based on information in the passage. The other statement is an incorrect, or faulty, inference. Label the statements C for *correct* inference and F for *faulty* inference.

_____ a. This story takes place a long time ago.

_____ b. Ravi enjoyed learning martial arts.

_____ c. Ravi's instructors would let him advance to the third stage that day.

5. Understanding Main Ideas

One of the statements below expresses the main idea of the passage. One statement is too general, or too broad. The other explains only part of the passage; it is too narrow. Label the statements M for *main idea*, B for *too broad*, and N for *too narrow*.

_____ a. Martial arts help people develop self-control and concentration.

_____ b. There are more than a hundred marmas, or vital points.

_____ c. Ravi, a fourteen-year-old boy, had passed through two stages of martial arts and wanted to enter the third stage.

Correct Answers, Part A _____

Correct Answers, Part B _____

Total Correct Answers _____

24　A　Fill 'er Up

Are you tempted to buy a high octane gasoline for your car because you want to improve its performance? If so, take note: most cars do not need a high octane gasoline to perform properly and efficiently. In fact, experts estimate that only about 10 percent of cars on the road require high octane gasoline.

To find out what octane your engine needs, check your owner's manual for the recommended octane level. The recommended level is often regular unleaded (87 octane). Purchase the lowest octane gasoline that your car can use without knocking. Higher octane gas costs more and consumes more energy to produce at the refinery.

What are octane ratings? Octane ratings are a measure of the gasoline's ability to resist engine knock. The "knock" or "ping" in a engine results from the uneven burning of the compressed fuel-air mixture. Octane ratings, by law, must be posted on each gasoline pump with a bright yellow sticker. On dispensers for alternative automotive fuels, you will see different ratings that must be posted with a bright orange sticker. If you're using the recommended octane and your car's engine is not knocking, you may still want to test whether you are buying gasoline with an octane rating higher than necessary. Try using a lower octane gasoline. When the engine begins to knock, go up to the next octane level.

You do not need a higher octane gasoline if your car engine currently runs without making a knocking or pinging sound. If your car knocks or pings after you have followed the owner's manual recommendations about octane ratings, consider getting a tune-up. Your owner's manual will recommend a tune-up schedule, or your maintenance mechanic can tell you when a tune-up is necessary. If knocking occurs after a tune-up, try switching to a slightly higher octane gasoline. Initially, you may want to try a higher octane gas every other tankful to see whether the knocking is eliminated.

Using gasoline with too low an octane rating, however, can result in loss of power and even engine damage. High-performance engines, for example, may need a higher octane gasoline to keep them from knocking. With some engines, the octane requirement increases gradually with age.

Be aware that octane ratings of gasoline marked "premium" or "regular" are not always consistent. Your best bet is to check the octane rating posted on the yellow sticker at the pump.

Reading Time _____

Recalling Facts

1. High-octane gasoline is required in
   - ❏ a. only a small number of cars.
   - ❏ b. most cars on the road.
   - ❏ c. trucks and vans.

2. A car running on regular unleaded gas does not require a higher-octane gasoline if
   - ❏ a. the engine starts easily.
   - ❏ b. the car gets good mileage.
   - ❏ c. the engine runs without knocking or pinging.

3. Octane ratings measure
   - ❏ a. an engine's performance level.
   - ❏ b. energy consumption.
   - ❏ c. the gasoline's ability to resist engine knock.

4. Engine damage may result from
   - ❏ a. using gasoline with too high an octane rating.
   - ❏ b. using gasoline with too low an octane rating.
   - ❏ c. driving too slowly.

5. Gasoline marked "regular"
   - ❏ a. may not always have the same octane rating.
   - ❏ b. always has the same octane rating.
   - ❏ c. is usually at least 100 octane.

Understanding Ideas

6. A car engine that knocks or pings
   - ❏ a. must need a high-octane gasoline.
   - ❏ b. may need a tune-up.
   - ❏ c. is probably an older car.

7. Octane ratings are designed to
   - ❏ a. help the consumer buy the appropriate gasoline.
   - ❏ b. confuse the consumer.
   - ❏ c. improve engine performance.

8. The article suggests that using high-octane gas in most cars
   - ❏ a. is a good idea.
   - ❏ b. may actually be harmful.
   - ❏ c. is an unnecessary expense.

9. You can conclude from the article that high octane gas costs more because it
   - ❏ a. burns less oil.
   - ❏ b. consumes more energy to produce at the refinery.
   - ❏ c. is scarce.

10. You can conclude from the article that the law requires posted octane ratings at gas stations so that
    - ❏ a. drivers will pay more at the pump.
    - ❏ b. consumers are protected from fraud.
    - ❏ c. tune-ups are not necessary.

Fuel? What Fuel?

Congratulations! You have a new electric car! You unplug it from its battery charger, hop in, and punch in your personal identification number. The motor begins to whine, and off you go. You can't go any great distance, because you have to recharge often, say, every 25 to 50 miles (40 to 80 kilometers), but you can travel at a respectable speed, up to 60 miles (97 kilometers) per hour.

As you drive along, you attract a lot of attention. That's because your car is hard to miss. People pull alongside and stare at you. Uh-oh, here comes a police officer. No, he just wants to ogle like everybody else.

You can't run out of gas because you aren't using any. But you can run out of juice. After a few days, though, you get used to coasting on hills to save power, and you're not as worried about getting stuck. Your new car won't take you on a long trip, but most people just run around town anyway, and your car is perfect for that—inexpensive to operate, once the initial costs are out of the way, and fun to drive. And best of all, your new car is environmentally friendly—no emissions to pollute the air.

1. Recognizing Words in Context

Find the word *ogle* in the passage. One definition below is a *synonym* for that word; it means the same or almost the same thing. One definition is an *antonym*; it has the opposite or nearly opposite meaning. The other has a completely different meaning. Label the definitions S for *synonym*, A for *antonym*, and D for *different*.

_____ a. ignore

_____ b. pass

_____ c. stare

2. Distinguishing Fact from Opinion

Two of the statements below present *facts*, which can be proved correct. The other statement is an *opinion*, which expresses someone's thoughts or beliefs. Label the statements F for *fact* and O for *opinion*.

_____ a. The electric car needs to be recharged.

_____ b. The electric car is fun to drive.

_____ c. The electric car can travel up to 60 miles (97 kilometers) per hour.

3. Keeping Events in Order

Label the statements below 1, 2, and 3 to show the order in which the events happened.

_____ a. The driver charges the battery.

_____ b. A police officer looks at the car.

_____ c. The driver punches in a PIN to start the car

4. Making Correct Inferences

Two of the statements below are correct *inferences,* or reasonable guesses. They are based on information in the passage. The other statement is an incorrect, or faulty, inference. Label the statements C for *correct* inference and F for *faulty* inference.

_____ a. Electric cars are a real possibility for the future.

_____ b. Electric cars will help cut gas consumption.

_____ c. Soon we will all be driving electric cars.

5. Understanding Main Ideas

One of the statements below expresses the main idea of the passage. One statement is too general, or too broad. The other explains only part of the passage; it is too narrow. Label the statements M for *main idea,* B for *too broad,* and N for *too narrow.*

_____ a. Automobile makers are experimenting with different kinds of cars.

_____ b. An electric car has to be recharged often, but it goes reasonably fast.

_____ c. Driving an electric car is a different, but rewarding, experience.

Correct Answers, Part A _____

Correct Answers, Part B _____

Total Correct Answers _____

25   A   Sicily

Sicily is the largest and most populous island in the Mediterranean Sea. It forms an autonomous region of Italy with several other islands. At the north-eastern corner of the island, the Strait of Messina separates it from mainland Italy. Its strategic location gives Sicily command of sea and air routes between southern Europe and Africa. Palermo, the capital and largest city, is a center for trade, commerce, and industry.

Mountains cover most of the northern part of the island. Flat landscape is found only along the coast. With intense volcanic activity, Sicily is subject to severe earthquakes. Mount Etna, the island's highest peak, is also Europe's largest active volcano. Winter rainfall ranges from about 20 inches (50 centimeters) on the plains to 50 inches (130 centimeters) in the mountains. Summers are dry and hot. Once covered with trees, the island is now less than 4 percent forested. Cutting down forests for agriculture and other uses has caused severe soil-erosion problems. Attempts are being made to reforest the land.

Farming and livestock raising are the chief occupations in Sicily. More than three-fourths of the island is cultivated, but yields are low. Vineyards and orchards of lemon, orange, tangerine, and olive trees flourish on the lower mountain slopes. Wheat, barley, corn, almonds, grapes, and some cotton are produced. Cattle, mules, donkeys, and sheep are raised. Many peasants do not own their farms. The majority of agricultural land is privately owned.

Sicily's isolation and distance from mainland Italy accounts, in part, for its economic underdevelopment. In the last few decades, however, there has been a marked expansion of heavy industries based on petroleum refining, natural gas, and chemicals. Other industries include salt extraction, wine making, textiles, shipbuilding and repair, fertilizers, and pharmaceuticals. Food-processing industries include vegetable and fish canning and the extraction of citric acid and essential oils. Sulfur mining, once Sicily's principal mining activity, has declined. Almonds, fruits, tomatoes, artichokes, and fish are major exports.

Sicily was colonized by the Greeks during the eighth century B.C. In the third century B.C., it became the first Roman province. Large quantities of grain were produced and sent to Italy. Normans conquered Sicily in the eleventh century. It was ruled by the House of Bourbon during the 1700s and 1800s. It also became a major center of revolutionary movements in the nineteenth century. In 1861, it was incorporated into the United Kingdom of Italy.

Reading Time _____

Recalling Facts

1. Sicily is located in
   - ❑ a. the Mediterranean Sea.
   - ❑ b. the northern corner of Italy.
   - ❑ c. the Atlantic Ocean.

2. Europe's largest active volcano is
   - ❑ a. Sicily.
   - ❑ b. Mount Etna.
   - ❑ c. Palermo.

3. Sicily's severe soil-erosion problems are mainly the result of
   - ❑ a. dry, hot weather.
   - ❑ b. volcanic activity.
   - ❑ c. felling forests.

4. Chief occupations in Sicily are
   - ❑ a. mining and shipbuilding.
   - ❑ b. wine making and fishing.
   - ❑ c. farming and livestock raising.

5. Sicily's first colonists were
   - ❑ a. Greek.
   - ❑ b. Roman.
   - ❑ c. Norman.

Understanding Ideas

6. The article wants you to understand that
   - ❑ a. Sicily will soon solve its problems.
   - ❑ b. Sicily suffers from many problems.
   - ❑ c. Sicily's problems are the result of its location.

7. The expansion of industries in Sicily will most likely
   - ❑ a. drain Sicily's resources.
   - ❑ b. interfere with development.
   - ❑ c. improve the island's economy.

8. You can conclude from the article that earthquake and volcano activity on Sicily
   - ❑ a. accounts for Sicily's isolation from mainland Italy.
   - ❑ b. is likely a hindrance to Sicily's development.
   - ❑ c. attracts tourists.

9. Palermo's reputation as a center of trade, commerce, and industry is no doubt due to
   - ❑ a. its government.
   - ❑ b. its location.
   - ❑ c. its population.

10. Three-fourths of Sicily is cultivated, but yields are low, which suggests that
    - ❑ a. better farming methods are needed.
    - ❑ b. farmers should work harder.
    - ❑ c. more land should be cultivated.

25   B   The Man Who United Italy

Originally a ship's captain, Giuseppe Garibaldi (1807–1882) was a brilliant military leader who fought for Italian independence from Austria in the 1850s. Forced to flee when European armies seized Italy, he had settled into private life as a farmer. But when political unrest again seized Italy, he raised his own army and successfully fought off the Austrians in 1859.

In the mid-1800s, the Sicilians were living under French rule and not liking it much. The island of Sicily had been handed back and forth from one European power to another. It had belonged to the Byzantine Empire, France, Italy, Spain, Austria, and France again. In 1860, the Sicilians rose up in rebellion. Garibaldi saw his chance. With 1,000 volunteers, he sailed from Genoa to join the Sicilian rebels against the French ruler. Garibaldi routed the French in an overwhelming victory. In 1861, the United Kingdom of Italy became a reality.

Everyone had thought Italian unification was impossible. For the first time, a unified Italy was within the grasp of the Italian people. They hailed Garibaldi as a hero. He became a national symbol of patriotism, and his deeds became legend. In Italy, he is still remembered as the man who unified Italy.

1. **Recognizing Words in Context**

   Find the word *routed* in the passage. One definition below is a *synonym* for that word; it means the same or almost the same thing. One definition is an *antonym;* it has the opposite or nearly opposite meaning. The other has a completely different meaning. Label the definitions S for *synonym,* A for *antonym,* and D for *different.*

   _____ a. directed

   _____ b. defeated

   _____ c. lost to

2. **Distinguishing Fact from Opinion**

   Two of the statements below present *facts,* which can be proved correct. The other statement is an *opinion,* which expresses someone's thoughts or beliefs. Label the statements F for *fact* and O for *opinion.*

   _____ a. Garibaldi fought for Italian independence.

   _____ b. The Sicilians rebelled in 1860.

   _____ c. Garibaldi was a brilliant general.

3. **Keeping Events in Order**

   Label the statements below 1, 2, and 3 to show the order in which the events happened.

   _____ a. Garibaldi defeated the French in Sicily.

   _____ b. The Sicilians were unhappy under French rule.

   _____ c. Italy became a unified country.

4. **Making Correct Inferences**

   Two of the statements below are correct *inferences*, or reasonable guesses. They are based on information in the passage. The other statement is an incorrect, or faulty, inference. Label the statements C for *correct* inference and F for *faulty* inference.

   _____ a. Sicily lived through centuries of political unrest.

   _____ b. The Italian people still honor Garibaldi's achievements.

   _____ c. Unification was not very important to the Sicilians.

5. **Understanding Main Ideas**

   One of the statements below expresses the main idea of the passage. One statement is too general, or too broad. The other explains only part of the passage; it is too narrow. Label the statements M for *main idea*, B for *too broad*, and N for *too narrow*.

   _____ a. Giuseppe Garibaldi contributed to the unification of Italy by defeating the French in Sicily.

   _____ b. Sicily's history is one of being handed from one European power to another.

   _____ c. Italian history includes much warfare.

Correct Answers, Part A _____

Correct Answers, Part B _____

Total Correct Answers _____

Answer Key

Reading Rate Graph

Comprehension Score Graph

Comprehension Skills Profile Graph

ANSWER KEY

1A	1. b	2. b	3. a	4. c	5. c	6. a	7. b	8. c	9. c	10. b
1B	1. S, A, D	2. F, F, O	3. S, S, B	4. C, F, C	5. M, N, B				
2A	1. c	2. b	3. b	4. c	5. b	6. a	7. a	8. c	9. c	10. b
2B	1. D, A, S	2. O, F, F	3. 3, 1, 2	4. C, F, C	5. N, B, M				
3A	1. c	2. b	3. b	4. c	5. a	6. b	7. a	8. c	9. b	10. a
3B	1. A, S, D	2. F, F, O	3. 1, 2, 3	4. C, F, C	5. B, N, M				
4A	1. a	2. b	3. c	4. b	5. c	6. b	7. a	8. c	9. a	10. b
4B	1. D, A, S	2. F, F, O	3. S, B, S	4. C, C, F	5. M, B, N				
5A	1. c	2. b	3. a	4. c	5. b	6. c	7. b	8. c	9. b	10. a
5B	1. S, A, D	2. F, O, F	3. B, S, S	4. C, C, F	5. M, N, B				
6A	1. b	2. c	3. c	4. b	5. b	6. a	7. b	8. a	9. c	10. b
6B	1. D, A, S	2. O, F, F	3. S, B, S	4. C, F, C	5. B, M, N				
7A	1. a	2. b	3. a	4. c	5. a	6. b	7. c	8. a	9. c	10. a
7B	1. A, S, D	2. F, F, O	3. 2, 3, 1	4. C, F, C	5. B, N, M				
8A	1. a	2. c	3. a	4. c	5. b	6. b	7. a	8. b	9. a	10. b
8B	1. S, D, A	2. O, F, F	3. S, A, S	4. F, C, C	5. N, M, B				
9A	1. b	2. a	3. c	4. a	5. c	6. a	7. b	8. b	9. a	10. c
9B	1. S, D, A	2. F, O, F	3. B, S, S	4. C, F, C	5. B, N, M				
10A	1. c	2. b	3. b	4. a	5. c	6. a	7. b	8. b	9. c	10. a
10B	1. A, D, S	2. F, F, O	3. S, S, A	4. F, C, C	5. B, N, M				
11A	1. b	2. c	3. c	4. b	5. a	6. c	7. a	8. a	9. b	10. c
11B	1. A, S, D	2. F, F, O	3. 2, 3, 1	4. C, F, C	5. B, N, M				
12A	1. b	2. a	3. b	4. c	5. c	6. c	7. b	8. b	9. c	10. a
12B	1. A, D, S	2. O, F, F	3. 2, 3, 1	4. C, C, F	5. M, B, N				
13A	1. a	2. b	3. a	4. b	5. c	6. b	7. c	8. a	9. b	10. b
13B	1. D, S, A	2. F, F, O	3. 3, 2, 1	4. F, C, C	5. N, B, M				

14A	1. b	2. b	3. a	4. c	5. a	6. b	7. b	8. c	9. b	10. c
14B	1. A, S, D	2. O, F, F	3. 1, 2, 3	4. C, F, C	5. M, B, N				
15A	1. b	2. a	3. b	4. c	5. a	6. b	7. b	8. a	9. a	10. c
15B	1. A, S, D	2. F, F, O	3. 3, 2, 1	4. C, F, C	5. B, N, M				
16A	1. a	2. c	3. c	4. b	5. a	6. b	7. a	8. b	9. b	10. c
16B	1. A, S, D	2. F, F, O	3. 1, 2, 3	4. C, F, C	5. B, N, M				
17A	1. c	2. c	3. b	4. a	5. b	6. a	7. b	8. a	9. c	10. a
17B	1. A, D, S	2. F, O, F	3. A, S, S	4. C, C, F	5. N, M, B				
18A	1. b	2. c	3. c	4. a	5. b	6. b	7. b	8. a	9. a	10. c
18B	1. S, A, D	2. F, O, F	3. 2, 1, 3	4. F, C, C	5. N, M, B				
19A	1. b	2. c	3. b	4. a	5. c	6. b	7. a	8. a	9. c	10. a
19B	1. D, A, S	2. F, F, O	3. 2, 1, 3	4. C, C, F	5. M, B, N				
20A	1. a	2. b	3. c	4. c	5. b	6. a	7. a	8. c	9. a	10. b
20B	1. A, D, S	2. F, F, O	3. 2, 1, 3	4. C, C, F	5. N, B, M				
21A	1. b	2. a	3. b	4. b	5. c	6. b	7. c	8. a	9. a	10. c
21B	1. D, S, A	2. O, F, F	3. 3, 2, 1	4. C, F, C	5. N, M, B				
22A	1. c	2. a	3. b	4. a	5. b	6. a	7. b	8. a	9. c	10. a
22B	1. S, A, D	2. F, F, O	3. 3, 1, 2	4. C, C, F	5. M, B, N				
23A	1. b	2. b	3. a	4. b	5. c	6. c	7. c	8. b	9. b	10. a
23B	1. S, A, D	2. F, F, O	3. S, A, S	4. C, C, F	5. B, N, M				
24A	1. a	2. c	3. c	4. b	5. a	6. b	7. a	8. c	9. b	10. b
24B	1. A, D, S	2. F, O, F	3. 1, 3, 2	4. C, C, F	5. B, N, M				
25A	1. a	2. b	3. c	4. c	5. a	6. b	7. c	8. b	9. b	10. a
25B	1. D, S, A	2. F, F, O	3. 2, 1, 3	4. C, C, F	5. M, N, B				

READING RATE

Put an X on the line above each lesson number to show your reading time and words-per-minute rate for that unit.

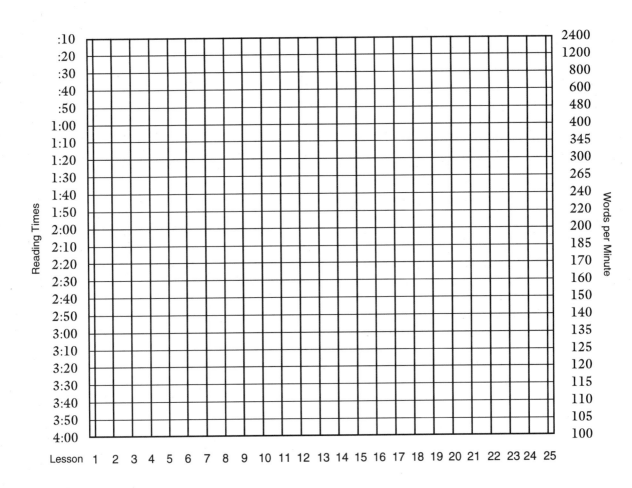

COMPREHENSION SCORE

Put an X on the line above each lesson number to indicate your total correct answers and comprehension score for that unit.

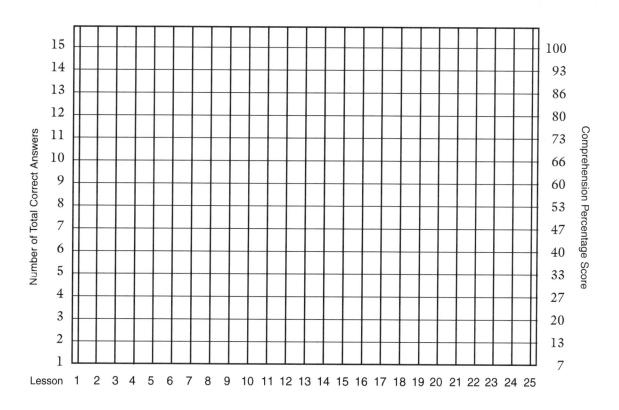

Comprehension Skills Profile

Put an X in the box above each question type to indicate an incorrect reponse to any part of that question.

Lesson 1					
2					
3					
4					
5					
6					
7					
8					
9					
10					
11					
12					
13					
14					
15					
16					
17					
18					
19					
20					
21					
22					
23					
24					
25					
	Recognizing Words in Context	Distinguishing Fact from Opinion	Keeping Events in Order	Making Correct Inferences	Understanding Main Ideas